ENGAGING
ADOLESCENTS
in
READING

ENGAGING ADOLESCENTS *in* READING

John T. Guthrie
Editor

CORWIN PRESS
A SAGE Company
Thousand Oaks, CA 91320

For information:

Corwin Press
A SAGE Company
2455 Teller Road
Thousand Oaks, California 91320
www.corwinpress.com

SAGE Ltd.
1 Oliver's Yard
55 City Road
London, EC1Y 1SP
United Kingdom

SAGE India Pvt. Ltd.
B 1/I 1 Mohan Cooperative
Industrial Area
Mathura Road, New Delhi 110 044
India

SAGE Asia-Pacific Pte. Ltd.
33 Pekin Street #02-01
Far East Square
Singapore 048763

Printed in the United States of America.

Library of Congress Cataloging-in-Publication Data

Engaging adolescents in reading / edited by John T. Guthrie.
    p. cm.
Includes bibliographical references and index.
ISBN 978-1-4129-5334-4 (cloth)
ISBN 978-1-4129-5335-1 (pbk.)

  1. Reading (Secondary)—United States. 2. Reading (Middle school)—United States. 3. Motivation in education—United States. I. Guthrie, John T. I. Title.

LB1632.E54 2008
428.4071'2—dc22

                                      2007040310

This book is printed on acid-free paper.

07 08 09 10 11 10 9 8 7 6 5 4 3 2 1

Acquisitions Editor: Cathy Hernandez
Editorial Assistants: Megan Bedell, Cathleen Mortensen
Production Editor: Appingo Publishing Services
Cover Designer: Rose Storey
Graphic Designer: Lisa Miller

Contents

Preface

The mission of this book is to open the window to a new understanding of reading motivation. Across the nation, teachers in secondary schools face unmotivated students daily in their classrooms. Presenting the supreme challenge to teachers, these students do themselves a disservice by adopting an oppositional stance to reading and writing. Despite the predominance of this dilemma, teachers are little informed by research on how to engage their students in long-term reading. In this book, we portray the spectrum of students' reasons for avoiding reading that pervade classrooms and schools. Likewise, we illuminate the students' feelings, reasons, and emotions for engaging in literacy.

This book aims to arm teachers with solutions to this dilemma. We depict five vital classroom practices for engaging adolescents in reading. Each practice is linked to a key motivational quality such as interest, ownership, confidence, collaboration, and the desire to understand texts fully. These approaches to teaching are deep, yet doable. Each motivational strategy can be initiated tomorrow in any subject matter that involves books and texts. Beyond one day, they can become the foundation of a renewed structure for teaching in a school. In contrast to the commonplace approach of helping adolescents by teaching them strategies for reading, what students need is motivation, and what teachers seek are ways to engage the passions and commitments of learners. Meeting teachers' profound needs for new hope is an aim of this book.

The knowledge base of this book is scientific. Since 2000, researchers in psychology, anthropology, linguistics, and education have joined forces to build a science of motivational development and how classrooms foster it. Above all, this scientific knowledge is based on experiments and quantitative studies. In the absence of field trials, we have speculation but no confirmed knowledge. Although hundreds of field trials for motivating students and engaging adolescents in reading have been published in the past decade, these fertile resources have not been accessible to teachers until this volume. More than two hundred journal articles of the highest scientific caliber have been fused into the framework of this book. Contributors to this book have read, digested, interpreted, synthesized, and portrayed the findings of this knowledge base superbly.

Written by teachers, with the collaboration of the editor, this book sparkles with concreteness. Voices of students and the stories of teachers permeate its pages. Vivid vignettes crafted by remarkable educators carry the messages of how teachers engage adolescents in reading. Not transitory flashes, these illustrations embody the deepest principles that flow from the knowledge base in motivational development and engagement in literacy. Within these pages, the reader can see how motivation looks to a teacher and how it feels to a student to be engaged in reading.

The audience for this volume begins with educators who are seeking to reach their students. Further, literacy leaders who refuse to accept the crisis of student disengagement that too often results from today's cloistered curricula will find potentials for change. Administrators who are dissatisfied with the current outcomes of high-stakes testing will be informed. Optimistic educators who expect that higher standards can be met through deeper engagement in reading will find their beliefs confirmed in this volume.

Literacy leaders in secondary schools increasingly demand to know the critical ingredients of instruction for reading improvement. This book discusses the textbooks, teaching frameworks, and student activities that enable learners to shift into becoming active readers. Associated with this volume are needs-assessment questionnaires and evaluation rubrics designed to guide schools toward a new literacy agenda. Policy makers at the school, district, and state levels can take the directions recommended for engaging all learners in literacy. Just as expertise in music or sports is not an overnight happening, high school reading achievement is a long-term venture. The blueprints for beginning that journey and sustaining its progress are enclosed in these pages.

Educational practices at the heart of this volume are contained in Chapters 2 through 6. The opening chapter establishes the need for attention to engagement in reading. Chapter 2 focuses on helping students read deeply, which is astonishingly infrequent in today's classrooms. Because meaning is motivating to learners, this chapter gives practical steps for endowing books with significance. Chapter 3 addresses students' needs to take charge of their lives and their literacy. We show how teachers give choices that boost students' investment without distracting them from the heart of the curriculum. In Chapter 4, ways to tap adolescents' social motivations through group work are addressed. Chapter 5 places students' confidence at the center. Although the gap between student achievement and textbook demands is often five years or greater, leading students to feel helplessness, teacher actions can bridge the student-textbook abyss.

In Chapter 6, we exploit the potency of relevance to increase students' interests in book reading. When students see the book, the text, or the assignment as personally significant, they make an investment and, with it, their interest rises. Chapter 7 tours students' motivational growth, and Chapter 8 examines the motivational needs of struggling readers. In Chapter 9, we plot the next steps for teachers who seek to transform their classrooms. Using self-monitoring questionnaires for teachers and students, teachers can form inquiry groups in schools and districts. By initiating these next steps, teachers' expectations for reaching all students can attain a new level of optimism.

Acknowledgments

My personal background is the educational psychology of reading, its processes, and its improvement in classrooms. For the focus on motivation, I owe a debt of gratitude to my colleague, Allan Wigfield, a motivation expert, for 15 years of collaboration and delightful seminars with students.

Graduate students at the University of Maryland helped enormously in forging the linkage of research to the practices of teaching in my mind and in this volume. While there are others, I especially thank Emily Anderson Swan, Kathleen Cox Perencevich, Ana Taboada, Marcia H. Davis, Angela Comment McRae, Cassandra Shular Coddington, Judy Huei-Yu, Stephen M. Tonks, Susan Lutz Klauda, Laurel Wagner Hoa, Nicole M. Humenick, Nicole T. Scafiddi, and Meridith Villa Sloan for their questions, intuitions, and commitments.

In many chapters, we bring to light the experiences of our teacher colleagues. For the excerpts from their classrooms, we thank David J. Douglass, Allison L. Erdman, Robert K. Forney, Melissa Griffith, Suzanne Mentz, Megan Scott Tomas, Amanda Wells, and Christopher Ellis, and Paula Beth Segal, master's degree recipient.

I am especially obliged to Ellen M. Kaplan for her editorial expertise and contributions to the flow and organization of this book. My administrative assistant, Eileen Kramer, also contributed throughout.

I am grateful to my spouse, Stacey, who tolerated many hours away from the real action of a sabbatical in the mountains, when this book was edited, which includes hiking, canoeing, bird watching, sailing, watching sunrises, and reading novels.

The book was written and edited during the tenure of a six-year study of engagement and motivation for reading sponsored by the National Science Foundation. The work reported herein was supported by the Interagency

Educational Research Initiative (IERI: Award #0089225) as administered by the National Science Foundation. The findings and opinions expressed here do not necessarily reflect the position or policies of the Interagency Educational Research Initiative, the National Science Foundation, or the University of Maryland.

Publisher's Acknowledgments

Corwin Press gratefully acknowledges the contributions of the following individuals:

Maryann Baldwin, Counselor and AP Coordinator
Chamberlain High School, Tampa, FL

Kathy Corcoran, Literacy Coach
Pajaro Valley Unified School District, Watsonville, CA

Vicki Seeger, Literacy Coach
Indian Creek Elementary School, Topeka, KS

About the Editor

John T. Guthrie is the Jean Mullan Professor of Literacy in the Department of Human Development at the University of Maryland, College Park. As director of the Maryland Literacy Research Center, he studies motivations and strategies in reading at all school levels. Before coming to Maryland, he was research director for the International Reading Association. He began his career at Johns Hopkins University, where he founded the Kennedy School for children with reading disabilities. His works on reading engagement have been published in the *Reading Research Quarterly*, the *Journal of Educational Psychology*, and the *Elementary School Journal*. He is a recipient of the Oscar Causey Award for Outstanding Reading Research, a member of the International Reading Association Hall of Fame, and the 2004 recipient of the University of Maryland System Regents' Award for research/scholarship/creative activity.

About the Contributors

Dee Antonio teaches International Cultures & Cuisines, Food Trends, and Technology, and Child Development at Rockville High School in Rockville, Maryland. She holds a master's degree in education from the University of Maryland, College Park, with a focus on minority students' behaviors and attitudes, and a BS in human ecology from the University of Maryland, Eastern Shore, with a concentration in family and consumer sciences education. She is head coach of Rockville High School's indoor track-and-field team and assistant coach of the outdoor track-and-field team. She is an active member of the Black Leaders in Action organization.

Jessica E. Douglass is currently teaching English in Poolesville, Maryland. She earned her undergraduate degree in education from The Pennsylvania State University and her graduate degree in health and human development from The University of Maryland. She has been instrumental in developing a new curriculum for The Poolesville High School Humanities House, making connections between the American authors studied in English class to the historical context explored in U.S. history. She leads her students in viewing the texts through the historical, social, and economic perspectives in which they are written.

Sarah Fillman currently teaches 10th- and 12th-grade English at Montgomery Blair High School in Silver Spring, Maryland, where she also coaches the varsity cheerleading team. She has a master's degree in human development from the University of Maryland, College Park. In addition to her love for teaching literature and writing, Sarah enjoys studying psychology, specifically, mixing psychotherapy with exercise therapy as a means of managing stress. Her hobbies include exercising, reading, and making jewelry.

Robert L. Gibb currently teaches AP European History and Modern World History at Montgomery Blair High School. During his 18-year career at this Silver Spring, Maryland, institution, he has worked primarily with "at-risk" students in an effort to establish within them a renewed interest and sense of value in their education. In addition to his teaching responsibilities, he also coaches Girls Varsity Soccer and Boys Varsity Lacrosse. He is a National Board Certified Teacher and recently received a master's degree in education (human development) from the University of Maryland, College Park. Mr. Gibb resides with his daughter, Kinsey, in Silver Spring, Maryland.

Lucas M. Henry teaches 10th-grade English and AP English at Montgomery Blair High School in Silver Spring, Maryland. He received his master's degree in education from the University of Maryland and a BA in secondary education from American University, with a concentration in English. He is interested in the use of computer-based reading programs.

Sandra Jacobs Ivey currently teaches 12th-grade English at Montgomery Blair High School in Silver Spring, Maryland. She began her 18-year teaching career in the District of Columbia at a PreK–8 open school, followed by junior high and middle school, before settling into the culturally diverse Blair in 1998. Additionally, she has taught Spanish in elementary school and ESOL for both adolescent and adult learners. Formally trained using the Junior Great Books Inquiry Model and as a Socratic Seminar leader, Ivey is committed to helping students develop essential literacy skills. Ivey received her master's in education from the University of Maryland.

Shana Yudowitch currently teaches 9th-grade Matter and Energy (a physical science course) and 10th-grade biology at Colonel Zadok Magruder High School in Montgomery County Public Schools, Maryland. Before teaching, she earned her undergraduate degree in secondary science education at the University of Maryland. Currently she holds the position of Matter and Energy team leader and has earned her master's of education degree in the field of human development at the University of Maryland. It is her ambition to pursue national certification and to continue as a classroom teacher.

1

Reading Motivation and Engagement in Middle and High School

Appraisal and Intervention

John T. Guthrie
University of Maryland

This chapter sets the stage for our approach to motivation and engagement in middle and high school reading. First, we portray the dilemmas. Students read too little, and they rarely read for deep understanding. They seldom read to expand their sense of who they are as people. Faced with students who are less than ideally motivated, teachers often attempt to control behavior and get through the day. With so many responsibilities, teachers too rarely provide instructional support for reading engagement. A range of new research, however, yields insights about students' needs and teachers' actions. Our second goal is to introduce the teaching practices that can work. Throughout the book, we depict examples for classrooms or whole school initiatives.

● 1

Dilemmas of Students' Motivation and Engagement in School Reading

Reading in high school is tied tightly to motivation. A majority of Advanced Placement (AP) students are motivated readers. However, many on-grade level, slightly below-grade level, or seriously deficient students are demotivated, apathetic, or expressly resistant to reading school content. Too many students report that they seldom do homework, that their minds drift in class, and that they do not see reading as functional to their future lives. A majority of students have little interest in reading for pleasure. At least half believe that they cannot read proficiently enough to understand the textbooks they use daily in classes. Alarming as they appear, these claims are buttressed by ample evidence.

In 2003, a nationally representative sample of Grade 12 students took a survey about their reading engagement (Grigg, Daane, Jin, & Campbell, 2003). Students answered questions such as, "How often do you read something for school?" with possible responses of "Every day," "A few times a week," "Once a week," or "About once a month." The responses were astonishing. A huge majority of 12th graders (93%) reported that they did not read every day for school. The bulk of the most extreme nonreaders had already dropped out of school and did not respond to the survey. A substantial majority (69%) did not read for enjoyment. This is a problem, because reading for enjoyment is a signal of intrinsic motivation, which refers to reading for its own sake.

An abundance of statistical research shows that intrinsic motivation drives students' amount of reading. Students who read for internal reasons (interest, pleasure, favorite topics) read a lot and achieve highly. In contrast, students who read only for external reasons, such as grades, rewards, or recognition, do not read as often or as deeply. These are not mere notions or subjective impressions. They are well-verified conclusions from extensive, carefully designed interviews, questionnaires, and diary studies (see Table 1.1: Stanovich & Cunningham, 1992; Wigfield & Guthrie, 1997).

Some would say that adolescents across the globe are disinterested in reading for school. Perhaps, but in a comparison of fifteen-year-old students

Table 1.1   Grade 12 Students' Reading for School and Enjoyment

Questions	Percentage Agreed
Do not read daily for school	93%
Rarely read science articles, history sources, or textbooks	74%
Almost never read for own enjoyment	69%
Reading is not a favorite activity	66%
Do not read a book from the library more than once a month	62%

across the globe, U.S. students showed low reading engagement. In an extensive international survey in 2000, fifteen-year-olds reported how much time they read for enjoyment, the breadth and depth of the books and magazines they read, and their level of reading interest. Together, these qualities were merged into an index of "reading engagement." United States students ranked 20th out of 28 developed countries on this reading engagement index, lower than Finland, Norway, Germany, France, Japan, Canada, Korea, and the list of countries goes on (Kirsch et al., 2002). In this survey, U.S. students were 24th out of 28 countries on the proportion who were "book readers," as contrasted with "magazine readers," "newspaper readers," and "light fiction readers." Thus, the United States did not show well in that international comparison of reading engagement and motivation.

We might not have cause for concern if reading engagement and motivation were merely recreational. But these qualities contribute to achievement in reading. (Guthrie, Hoa, Wigfield, Tonks, Humenick, & Littles, 2007). In the Program for International Student Assessment (PISA) comparison, students' reading engagement predicted achievement on a test of reading comprehension in every nation tested, including the United States. Also, students' reading interest predicted their reading comprehension in every country.

Remarkably, reading engagement was more important than students' family background consisting of parents' education and income. Reading engagement connected to achievement more strongly than to home environment. Students with high reading engagement, but lower parental education and income, had higher reading achievement than students with lower reading engagement and the same background characteristics did. In this study and others, reading engagement trumped socioeconomic status as a correlate of reading achievement (Guthrie, Schafer, & Huang, 2001). No one is claiming that this is a causal relationship. Reading engagement and reading achievement interact in a spiral. Higher achievers read more, and the more engaged these students become, the higher they achieve. Likewise, lower achievers read less, and the less engaged decline in achievement. The spiral goes downward as well as upward. In fact, continued low engagement is a precursor to dropping out of school (Finn & Rock, 1997). Thus, engagement is not benign.

Disengagement from reading has its roots in earlier years. According to a nationally representative survey of fourth graders in 2005, 65% of students did not report reading as a favorite activity. In the same survey, 73% of students did not read frequently for enjoyment, and 59% of students stated that they did not believe that they learned very much when reading books. In our judgment, reading as a favorite activity and reading for enjoyment are indicators of intrinsic motivation for reading. These statistics indicate that a substantial majority of Grade 4 students are not intrinsically motivated to read. Data from the National Assessment of Educational Progress (NAEP) further show that students' intrinsic motivation, according to these indicators, decreased from 2002 to 2005 (Donahue, Daane, & Yin, 2005).

Compared to students in other countries, fourth graders in the United States are astonishingly low in intrinsic motivation for reading. A 2001 nationally representative sample of fourth graders from 35 countries ranked the United States 33rd in an index of students' attitudes toward reading (Mullis, Martin, Gonzalez, & Kennedy, 2003). In reading for their own interest outside of school, an indicator of intrinsic reading motivation, the U.S. students ranked 32nd. Students from the United States were equally unlikely to choose stories, novels, or reading for information outside of school. In a reanalysis of these data with a different coding scheme by independent investigators, U.S. students were found to be ranked 35th out of 35 countries in the revised index of attitudes toward reading. Though we should be cautious in interpreting the data from the lowest achievers due to unreliability in the measures, the apparent demotivation of U.S. students is nevertheless alarming (Gnaldi, Schagen, & Twist, 2005; Twist, Gnaldi, & Schagen, 2004).

In this book we are referring to school reading. Encompassing the interaction with fiction, literature, science, history, current events, personal narratives, Internet texts, and personal journals, this is no small domain. What distinguishes this domain from out-of-school reading is the premium that is placed on the goals of gaining knowledge, using text for improving other skills such as math or historical thinking, exchanging thoughts and opinions with peers, and aesthetic enjoyment of literature or of well-formed ideas. Out-of-school reading often centers on social interactions and is likely to feed personal pursuits or popular culture (Alvermann, 2001). Clearly, students can be engaged in nonschool literacy without being engaged in academic reading. But it is the frequency and depth of academic reading that associates positively and highly with measured reading comprehension, whereas nonschool reading (e.g., magazine reading) associates negatively with tested comprehension among adolescents both in the United States and in other countries (Kirsch et al., 2002). Our aim here is to explore the dynamics of school reading and its cultivation in the classroom.

Challenge: Teacher Support for Motivation and Engagement

Why are so many students disengaged from school reading? Without a doubt, lack of parental support, Internet distractions, and students' gainful employment are contributing factors. In addition, classrooms are a major source of disaffection with reading. Although motivation is not created in a week, students are highly sensitive to the classroom context. If a single teacher affords her students a certain number of well-designed choices in their reading, students respond with a bit more investment to those reading tasks. It is unrealistic to expect one teacher's actions to spread motivation throughout a student's life. However, within the microworld of one classroom, the motivational context matters. If this is true, how do students experience reading in high school?

Across our nation, U.S. students in Grade 12 took a questionnaire in 1998 and 2002. Combining across these, we present a portrait of student perceptions. This is a tip of the iceberg, but an important one. Table 1.2 shows results of threats to students' reading activities in response to questions such as, "When you are given reading assignments in class, how often do you have time to read books you have chosen?" Additional questions and their results are given in the table. Students answered either "Daily," "Weekly," "Several times a month," "Monthly," or "Never."

In this survey, students reported that in science and history classes, they almost never read books other than the textbook. While seemingly normal, this is actually problematic. Textbooks in these subjects are extremely difficult and are beyond the reach of all but the most advanced readers. Confronted with such texts, students suffer low self-efficacy when they try to read. In response, teachers often shelve the textbooks, and students are deprived of the knowledge they contain.

Students also reported that they rarely work in groups to understand the books in school. Restricting reading to an individual activity disadvantages many students who are disposed to social interaction and who need discussion to learn. Students are almost never given opportunities to

Table 1.2 Motivation Threats to School Reading Activities

Stem for all questions:		
"When you are given reading assignments in class, how often do you..."		

Questions	Percentage Agreed	Motivation Threatened
Read other than textbook for science	35	Self-efficacy
Read other than textbook for social studies	38	Self-efficacy
Work in groups to talk about text	35	Social interaction
Do a group project about what you read	29	Social interaction
Have time to read books you have chosen	18	Choice and control
Use library to borrow books for school	14	Choice and control
Have teacher help you break words into parts	23	Self-efficacy
Have teacher help you understand new words	55	Self-efficacy

choose books that are central to their academic learning. For example, 82% reported that teachers never give them time to read books they choose, and 86% reported that they never select books from the library for school reading. The table shows the numbers from this nationally representative sample of 12th graders.

This profile shows that students report *rarely* reading outside of the textbook, *seldom* collaborating with other students to interpret books, and *infrequently* choosing a text, a book, or a reading selection for schoolwork. This pattern raises barriers to motivation development because students require support for self-efficacy (through using readable texts), social interaction (through collaborating to read), and self-direction (through guidance in making good choices about reading).

In contrast to these instructional practices, students say that they usually experience a different set of teacher-directed reading activities. On the same questionnaires (Grigg et al., 2003; Levine, Rathbun, Selden, & Davis, 1998), 12th-grade students said that they were likely to do the following on a daily or weekly basis: (1) read silently in school (74%), (2) explain understanding of what you read to the class (65%), (3) have a class discussion of what you read (62%), (4) write about what you read (61%), or (5) make a class presentation about something you read (54%). Thus, a majority of 12th-grade students say they read silently, have class discussions, and write about what they read. Although these are sensible practices, they are not highly motivating. Such a pattern shows that reading is mostly textbook driven, teacher controlled, and content centered. Insufficient attention is paid to students' needs for making choices (being in control), showing competence (experiencing self-efficacy), and socially engaging with text (feeling related and belonging), all of which enable students to become motivated, engaged readers.

Although teachers often "inherit" highly motivated or unmotivated students from past classrooms and teachers, students are also sensitive to the context of a single classroom. Motivation for a course is not determined solely by home characteristics, or by the innate quality of being an avid learner. Within limits, the learning environment a teacher creates counts for students' motivation. Next, we overview students' reading motivations and how teachers can influence them, which is the subject of this book.

Meaning Is Motivating: Classroom Goal Structures

If students view the classroom as emphasizing understanding the main ideas, they become internally motivated. When students think that the teacher is devoted to their learning, they will read deeply. In contrast, when students perceive the teacher as bent on giving tests, checking scores, comparing students to each other, and striving exclusively toward external accountabilities, they become extrinsically motivated. These students will read for the test, but not for their own learning. They will seek the gold star, but not the comprehension of content. They will cheat, if necessary, to attain their goals and will minimize their efforts. On the other hand, when the teacher sets and sustains a context for engaged reading, students will grow intrinsically motivated and become invested in literacy learning.

Faced with a classroom of students who resist the text, teachers usually resort to coercion. Teachers often attempt to compel students to read under the threat of frequent testing. In the forms of weekly quizzes, daily writing tasks, and end-of-course grades, teachers demand compliance. Under a state of coercion, students' commitment to reading is undermined. Just at the age when students seek to be competent and independent, teachers are increasing their controls, constraints, and the regulation of students' school lives. Consequently, students rebel by not reading, not doing their homework, not paying attention in class, or not coming to class.

Control and Choice: Supporting Self-Directed Reading

It is self-evident that teachers cannot turn every page for every student in middle school and high school. Students become self-directing or they fail. Explicitly helping students to become self-directed is a charge to all teachers. Many teachers do it implicitly, without plans and conferences. Others either deliberately or unintentionally neglect this real need.

Enabling students to control significant elements of their reading and writing work is motivating. This refers to affording students significant choices in their reading. English teachers often allow students a choice of one of two short stories to read and critique. In history, effective teachers can allow students to select one of two sides of a controversial issue for reading and learning. In science, teachers can enable students to choose a subtopic for closer inspection in specialized reading. In these situations, students can determine how they will display their knowledge, or how they will express their understanding of text-based material.

Fortunately, teachers do not have to teach students to want choice. Students desire self-direction and control over their lives, especially in secondary school. Students seek more freedoms rather than fewer. The teacher's role is usually not to inspire students to prefer choice. Rather, the teacher's role is to provide their students with academically significant and realistic choices. Effective teachers expand students' liberties and levels of self-direction as the lesson, unit, and course proceed over time.

Teachers can make the simple commitment of affording one choice per day to the whole class. As a teacher, ask yourself, "What choice am I giving in period X today?" If a teacher has three above-grade level classes, then she probably already uses an expansive set of options, alternatives, and choices. She can likely continue, and even expand, these alternate pathways.

If a teacher has one on-grade class and two below-grade classes, she may think that choice is impossible. Compared to the liberties given to the above-grade students, she is correct. But when choice is tailored to their capacities, all students can benefit. For example, on a given day in an on-grade history class, a teacher can enable students to choose whether to read first about topic A (economy of ancient Egypt) or read first about topic B (religion of ancient Egypt), assuming the order is immaterial to the subject matter. Even this opportunity lends students a larger investment in the reading task. Such microchoices accumulate over time in their benefit for students' commitment. While not transforming a class into Egyptologists, one choice on one day can benefit students and begin a process of escalating engagement.

For a below-grade class in history, the teacher may give students the choice of writing one significant question for one page of text, and then have other students answer the question. This student-generated questioning gives each learner a sense of ownership (that was *my* question on *my* topic) when performed several times on different pages, with increasing success. Students may gain self-efficacy for a reading strategy (questioning increases comprehension) as a bonus. Effective motivation is not segregated from significant content. It is not motivation now and learning later. To the contrary, student motivation for deep reading is likely to develop when teachers fuse self-direction into lessons.

Reading Is Social: Bringing Peer Interaction to the Text

Students' social needs extend beyond their parties, pranks, chats, and fun. Students have a need for what researcher Ed Deci (1992) termed *relatedness*. They seek to be connected to a social network that will sustain them in the challenges of reading for school. At the center of the network is the teacher, who students see as a powerful force that they hope will become a personal ally. Students are motivated when they believe that teachers know them well enough to help them learn. If an individual student thinks that a certain teacher knows his interests in general, or in the topic of the course, that student is noticeably more invested in learning and reading. Feeling related to the teacher shores up a student's commitment to reading engagement (Skinner, Wellborn, & Connell, 1990).

Students often want to be cooperative with the teacher, classroom routines, and classmates. These individuals are termed *prosocial* by researcher Kathy Wentzel (1996). They seek to succeed in the class and want the social structure of the class to work well. These students are aware that a smoothly functioning classroom and individual student achievement often go hand in hand. Prosocial students are usually part of the social flow and academic success.

Accompanying students' social goals are their interactions around text. When teachers are able to build social interaction around course topics, students learn better. In English, when students honestly exchange viewpoints about central points in literature, their achievement in English increases (Applebee, Langer, Nystrand, & Gamoran, 2003). Beyond the benefits to tested achievement, students who experience these discussions gain deeper insight into literary nuances. They write with more astute self-knowledge than students who do not have opportunity for social interaction around reading. Often, group work in classrooms is not productive because it is not adequately goal driven, is insufficiently text based, or is not closely monitored. Yet there are structures for cooperative learning that are highly productive for reading improvement.

Self-Efficacy: Building Confident Readers

When students are faced with texts in which they understand few words, cannot read a paragraph aloud fluently, and understand little from a single page, they despair. Students know that they are failing at the most central school event: reading a book. This situation makes some students doubt their promise for success in school. In a state of low self-efficacy, students naturally resist the tasks that have punished them.

For students in grades ten to twelve, the typical gap between the textbook they have for class and the reading level they bring to the textbook is two to four years. In many cases, for science, history, and literature, the text is at a 12th-grade level, while students' reading comprehension is at an 8th- or 9th-grade level. Administrators or instructional leaders who doubt this need only to test the grade level of students compared to the readability levels of textbooks. Alternatively, they could poll teachers about the actual levels of students' reading.

When students are faced with texts two to four years beyond their reading level, they lose self-efficacy. Their confidence in their ability to learn from the text or from the course diminishes. Under these conditions, students find the course meaningless, and they become resistant, perhaps to their education in general. Thus, a learning dilemma that began as a gap between the text and the student becomes an abyss between the motivational dispositions of the learner and the curriculum goals of the school.

In English, the challenge of finding readable literature is serious, but can be addressed. Easier stories, high-interest books, and young adult fiction can be located. We do not advocate that the curriculum should be confined to texts on the pop culture of drugs, sex, and fantasy. But high-interest, low-difficulty books can represent at least a portion of the mainstream curriculum for all students.

In history, the use of multiple texts is a tradition. Students use a range of materials, including original sources, in attempting to form interpretations. Although some texts may be formidable, others such as newspaper accounts can be used as text for reading instruction and history education. Most challenging is the field of science. In some domains, such as life science and earth science, trade books are flourishing, and teachers may incorporate them as replacements for traditional textbooks or as substitutes for major topics in the curriculum.

The procedure for selecting effective texts is simple: Identify the reading level of the students via standardized reading tests, identify readable books based on a readability formula or judgments by teacher teams, and match the books with the students. Administrative investments in such matching will yield high returns in the effectiveness of reading lessons, content learning, and students' investment in their literacy development.

Interest in Reading: Potency of Relevance

Students at the secondary level seek competence. They want to be knowledgeable about the world around them and about the topics within the curriculum. Yet curriculum structures often thwart students' desire to gain expertise. When curricula are too broad, with too many topics addressed too briefly and with too few links to students' experiences and background understandings, students are unable to gain deep knowledge. Students are unable to talk about what they know, to apply their information about history, science, or English literature. Because their knowledge is only "school deep," students cannot use it outside of the lesson in which they learned it.

The most compelling way to address the dilemma posed by breadth of curriculum topics is to be thematic in content designs. Focus on what is central to the substantive discipline. Emphasize the big ideas. Is tone a "big idea" in 10th-grade English? If not, then underplay the role of tone and increase the role of such issues as theme and character development. Is a specific laboratory procedure the big idea in a high school physics course? Not likely. Then emphasize the big ideas. Acceleration, mass, and force are major concepts, yet many high school science classes are devoted to laboratory techniques and procedures. If students fail to grasp the major themes, they have no context for the techniques or procedures. Under these conditions, science reading becomes a word-recognition activity, rather than a conceptual understanding activity.

Students have extremely high needs for relevance. A relevant text is intrinsically motivating because it is "related to me." Students need to be able to apply their prior knowledge and their previous experience to texts they encounter. They want to know how a text or a subject matter relates to their real world and their prior learning. In some curricula, Homer's *The Odyssey* is taught in 10th-grade English. While this odyssey is the adventure of an old man coming home from a war, high school students are young people moving out of their homes into the wider world. It is unlikely that adolescents will relate their experience to the tribulations of Odysseus. Thus, *The Odyssey* is usually viewed as irrelevant, homework goes undone, and the book lies unread.

In physics, most students' background knowledge from everyday experience conflicts with scientifically based information. Without special treatment, these misconceptions prevent students from grasping major ideas. Often, texts and teachers do not address the misconceptions students bring to topics, with the result that the lessons do not take and the texts are not recalled. To be motivating, literacy instruction requires an orchestration of the new text into students' existing knowledge. Without an exquisite balance between new and old, students do not see the relevance, and their motivation declines.

Reading comprehension is a process of connecting the text and the student's prior knowledge about the topic of the text. It is self-evident that if the student lacks prior knowledge, new knowledge cannot be built and reading comprehension is impossible. Therefore, the management of students' prior knowledge from lesson to lesson, section to section, text to text, and course to course is imperative if reading instruction is to succeed. A first step in literacy instruction is systematically setting content goals for reading.

Many high school classes in science, history, and literature, as well as those in other content areas such as foreign language, widely distribute a large number of semidetached topics across an academic year. When students are expected to learn everything about everything, they end up learning little about anything. Students cannot retain a list of disconnected facts from one day to the next. Because reading comprehension improves when depth of understanding is facilitated, students need to deeply grasp one historical event or one scientific principle through multiple readings, applications, discussions, and connections to other areas. Therefore, organizing facts into principles, concepts into main ideas, and ideas into major themes within the content domains is vitally important. When students deeply understand, they gain comprehension skills, as well as knowledge. In this light, either students will gain depth from an instructional text or they will gain nothing. They will pick up reading skills when they understand the text, but not when the text is opaque. Thus, too much breadth of curriculum works against improvements in reading.

Needless to say, students are test sensitive. Teachers who maintain relevance give learning assessments that reward deep understanding. These assessments focus on the use of diverse, appropriate texts, and on the use of productive reading comprehension strategies, and students will learn toward these ends. The opposite also prevails. If teacher assessments are trivial, students' learning is trivialized. If science tests center on vocabulary meanings, but not on deep understandings, students will focus on the words, but not on the laws of science. If English tests are measures of trivia, students will attend to them, but not to the essential themes of literature. Assessments, then, should be closely tied to the engaged reading activities that follow the principles described here. Such assessments must be cumulative across time in a course and across years in a subject matter.

Struggling Readers: Boosting Motivation in Low Achievers

The downward spiral of reading failure, low grades, diminishing motivation, and school dropout is too familiar. As struggling secondary students move into adulthood, their reading deficits are often associated with a lack of employment, incarceration, lack of civic awareness, poor health maintenance, and poverty. Conversely, the ultimate benefit of reading motivation is empowerment. Since reading plays a vital role both in and out of school, motivated readers have an advantage. Even students who are underachieving can use reading if they are motivated to do so. Reading is not all or nothing. A 10th-grade student who is two years below grade level can nevertheless read and learn from texts at this level. Ultimately, this student has opportunities to act upon what he reads. In ideal circumstances, he can gain knowledge and shape a strong sense of self. But this is rare. Most of these low-achieving students become discouraged and withdraw from active reading. Preventing the ravages of low motivation for this group is a vital goal for educators. This aim can be attained with the teacher tools forged in this book from the new research on reading engagement and motivation.

For struggling readers, three types of motivational profiles stand out. Resistance to reading is prominent for one group. These students actively avoid books, shun texts, neglect reading homework, and deny school literacy of most kinds. Admittedly, they may do text messaging and may immerse themselves in Internet videos that demand some thinking. But these literacies do not transfer well to school tasks. Resistant students suffer, especially because they do not gain any knowledge, information, or content from most courses. Their avoidance will flatline their knowledge growth and reading development.

Resistant students suffer a lack of connection between their texts and their experience. They little realize that text links to life in the past, present, or future. Abstract words, symbols, terms, titles, and propositions do not have any links to reality for these students. Without connecting to knowledge or experience, the text is quite meaningless. At the heart of reading is merging the new information with the existing information. In the absence of this merger, students fail to comprehend, and they become frustrated. Once they are aware of their deficiencies, their self-efficacy suffers. Caught on the downward spiral of declining self-efficacy and meaningless reading activities, students come to actively resist books. One can sympathize with their situation.

Reversing this spiral is a teacher's challenge. Yet a single teacher in a single classroom with a traditional curriculum is not likely to make headway quickly. Needed changes include more connections such as video linked to readable text. These students need success in content-relevant books to bolster their self-efficacy. They need choices about reading to advance their sense of ownership over reading. Collaborative learning from books is important. Unfortunately, traditional classroom routines may not lend themselves to these qualities, and new classes or units for resistant students must be planned and implemented.

A second group of struggling readers is extrinsically motivated. These students are moderately able to read, but have no interest in school topics. Lacking devotion, their reading is minimal and superficial (Meece & Holt, 1993). Although these students will complete reading tasks for a grade or to avoid punishment, they do not comprehend well enough to achieve highly. Despite their willingness to perform some tasks, they feel little ownership over reading or school learning.

Teachers can reach these students through affording students some choice, input into their learning, and opportunity to connect personal interest to academic topics. A student who is interested in reading only sports cannot quickly relate his interest to European history. However, the student will have more or less interest in various topics within European history. A choice of subtopics will enable him to read the more interesting rather than the less interesting ones. Thus, a modicum of self-direction and an increment of intrinsic motivation become possible. The downward spiral for this group can be reversed with support for self-direction and collaborative reading with peers.

A third group of struggling readers is the lowest achieving, at or below the Grade-3 level. These students need word-level skills in reading. Their belief in their abilities (self-efficacy) is low. In interviews, they offer that they cannot recognize words and so they cannot read, which is an accurate reflection of reality (Guthrie et al., in press). Their motivation for school reading cannot include interest, choice, or collaboration because they cannot decode words well enough. Consequently, careful training and/or tutoring in reading with an emphasis on word-level skills is imperative. Self-efficacy support is vital too. These students must experience success in easy reading tasks. Awareness of their accomplishment enables them to build up their self-concept as readers. With the acquisition of Grades 3 to 5 reading skills, intrinsic motivation and interest become possible. Many of these students can gain competencies that are functional for school. But they need nurturing for self-efficacy in reading and interest in topical texts to become self-determining readers.

Merging Engagement Support Into Structured Classroom Management

All classrooms require structures, rules, plans, and expectations. The schedules, curriculum objectives, testing requirements, and teacher accountabilities all require that students participate in an organized system that the teacher creates and enforces. Furthermore, there are costs to students who violate the system. To assure student compliance, many teachers—especially the less experienced—rely on the costs and punishments. For rowdy behavior, some teachers subtract points or give more homework. Some teachers warn that students who refuse to work cooperatively in a team project will take an additional quiz. Such controls have quick benefits in the short term. Students follow the commands and shift their behavior to avoid punishment.

Under these conditions, students are controlled, but the control is external. Coming from outside of the student, today's threat will control today's unruly behavior. But tomorrow that behavior returns. Only if goals, rules, and standards are internalized will students constructively participate in the system in the long term. When students take ownership of being classroom citizens, they will become positive members. Likewise, when students pick up internal reasons for reading (understanding, enjoyment, personal accomplishment), they will self-initiate reading behaviors. Thus, relying on punishments or loss of privileges for control has short-term effects. These practices are occasionally necessary for crisis intervention. But teachers who foster successful long-term engagement merge the practices of meaningful goals, choice, collaboration, self-efficacy support, and relevance into the web of rules for the classroom.

For example, the principle of "giving choice" must be placed in this *system* perspective. Most teachers in most courses and in most schools must follow a curriculum. Daily schedules, school testing accountability, and student needs for specific skills in specialized topics are ever present. However, although teachers do not decide whether to follow the curriculum, they usually have a fraction of within-curriculum flexibility. In English, teachers may be able to afford students choices such as which three of six available short stories to read in a unit. English teachers may be able to give students input into how texts and videos are viewed and interpreted in a unit on mythology. In history, teachers can give choices about which military leader to specialize in, or which side to take in a debate on a controversial issue.

Using such freedoms responsibly, students may select texts and modes of representing them. Teacher guidance in using these liberties must necessarily be provided. We are suggesting that support for students' autonomy can be fused into a lesson, a unit, and a course of study. Likewise, engagement-enhancing practices can be merged into a framework of structured teaching.

Throughout this book, we portray and recommend advancements in instruction. Simultaneously, we acknowledge reality. We do not inhabit utopian classrooms, nor do we proclaim that we should all move to an unrealistic system. Standards of achievement in various curriculum areas will be—and should be—maintained. Assessments for accountability are widespread, popular, and necessary in a publicly responsible education program, however poor the administration of testing may sometimes be. Modifying these forces is beyond the scope of this book. We do not hold sacred the current curriculum goals or the testing system, but we are not promulgating their upheaval either. We take the stance that dramatic improvements in students' engagement are feasible within the myriad of constraints that exist within our legally constituted education system. We suggest that both incremental and more foundational improvements are possible and necessary.

Next Steps: Transforming Classrooms and Schools

Teachers, reading specialists, and curriculum planners can take steps to improve engagement in their classrooms and schools. The first step is interchange. Educators should begin to talk about student engagement. Beyond the well-founded complaints, teachers can ask, "What kind of motivations do our students have?" To begin this conversation, start with a reading engagement survey. The survey is directed to both students and teachers. Students report their engagement by describing their reading motivations, including the following: mastery goals, preference for choice, social orientation, self-efficacy, and interest. These can be tailored to specific courses or grade levels.

On the instructional side, teachers can report their practices that support reading engagement. This includes the role of such practices as the following: classroom goals, choice, collaboration, text selection, and relevance. These surveys can be utilized to guide discussion among educators. They can be a framework for evaluating curriculum changes, and they can enable leaders to identify professional development needs.

Instructional improvement can be made at all levels. Within his classroom for one group of students, an individual teacher can act to shift toward more positive engagement. Teachers can enable students to form small, personal connections with text. One teacher opened her history unit on European foreign policy by asking students where they were on September 11. Following some memories, students debated what the United States should do about that attack. After an exchange of opinions, she let them know they were discussing foreign policy. She next showed how several student ideas were used by politicians in prior years in Europe. With that connection, the text came to life that day. On a broader scale, in systematic ways, teachers can motivate students to read. Inspiring teachers are doing it daily. But many teachers will benefit from interchange with others about how to advance students' reading engagement.

At a second level, grade-level teams within a school can talk. Perhaps grade-level, within-subject-matter teams are best in some schools. In this group, curriculum goals, student options, collaboration, and relevance can be explored. Shifts that may not affect the school or district commitment can be made to design a more energizing plan for engagement. Furthermore, some issues are best addressed at the schoolwide level. For instance, the book list in English, the textbook in biology, or the Web sites in history may be revisited with respect to their power to engage students in motivated reading. Can they be shifted, altered, or extended, or can choices be offered to students without upsetting other priorities? Is the school schedule working to enhance or undermine students' reading engagement? The engagement surveys and the implications of the findings can be used to shed light on these issues.

Many instructional directions are set at the district and state levels. With survey data, educational leaders can set goals, design curricula, construct evaluations, and provide professional development that responds to the reading engagement needs of students. Fortunately, improvements in the infrastructure for reading engagement will foster student achievement. By the criterion of accountability for raising reading achievement test scores, reading engagement works. The benefit is worth the cost for administrators to invest in districtwide reading engagement.

2

Meaning Is Motivating

Classroom Goal Structures

Jessica E. Douglass and John T. Guthrie
University of Maryland

To be successful in any subject matter, students must be motivated to be literate. On any given day, they need to understand the formula in their math texts, a short story in their English curriculum, a description of the digestive system for health class, or a conversation in a foreign language for Spanish class. Students are constantly expected to read material in any class; but what if they are not motivated? What if the final exam requires that they read an excerpt from The Constitution, the Emancipation Proclamation, and several letters to and from Abraham Lincoln in order to describe the reasons for the conclusion of the Civil War, but they have not done the reading? For students to achieve, they need to want to engage with myriad texts.

According to an international report on reading among fifteen-year-olds, interest in reading is a major indicator in scholastic performance (Artlet, Baumert, Julius-McElvany, & Peschar, 2003). In that study, engagement in reading correlated with reading achievement for fifteen-year-olds for all 35 countries including the United States (Kirsch et al., 2002). As teachers, once we are convinced of that, we face the dilemma of motivating students to want to improve their learning from text.

In research on motivation, investigators portray a student who wants to understand a text deeply, having a mastery goal for reading. This student does not seek to get by. She is not aiming merely to complete an assignment, to finish work, or to get a certain grade. She actually wants to conquer some content in her texts. In contrast, a student with a performance goal for reading is attempting to show a good behavior such as completing an assignment or getting a good grade. A performance-oriented student does not care whether he or she understands a text. Students with performance goals generally want to outperform others, look smarter than others, or gain extrinsic rewards such as grades (Stipek, 2002). Students with a performance-goal orientation limit the amount of effort they apply to learning and focus more on completing a task on time for a grade than taking the time to do it well.

As teachers, we aim to foster mastery goals rather than performance goals for our students' reading. How do we do this? The research on this issue makes a simple point. Teachers who put mastery goals into their teaching help students form mastery goals for learning. Though it sounds simple, this may not be so easy to apply. When we emphasize mastery goals in the classroom, we focus on "big ideas" and connections among topics. We push students to comprehend, explain, argue, transform, apply, and write about ideas from books, no matter what the specific topic is. Of course we grade their work, but we do not let them get obsessed with grades and undermine our mastery goals. Next, we present seven teaching practices we use to promote mastery motivation.

Our instructional practices begin with the obvious. First, *providing mastery goals* is a teacher's initial statement to the class that motivation is a high priority. Only if the teacher emphasizes such goals can the student incorporate them. Second, *making tasks relevant* is a key to establishing the base for understanding texts rather than memorizing (and then forgetting) them. Third, *using hands-on activities* enables students to link their sensory powers to the abstractions of a textbook. Fourth, assuring that students are *transforming text to meaning* helps them to gain interest. A meaningless text is inherently boring and not easily learned. Fifth, we spend time *scaffolding mastery motivation* because internal motivational development does not occur in a day but rather evolves over a unit or a year. Sixth, we organize to *provide reteach opportunities,* which enable students to take different paths to understanding. Seventh, we believe in *rewarding effort over performance* because this levels the playing field for all students to succeed in reading. Next, we explicate each of these.

Providing Mastery Goals

In our school district, as is becoming the trend across the nation, teachers are expected to post objectives for the students each day. The day's work should clearly be a step toward that goal of mastering a skill or understanding. When we do not post objectives and make it clear to students why the work is important, students will most often ask, "Why are we doing this?" It is best when we start class with the rationale for the work instead of scrambling for an answer to that question.

Mastery goals place a premium on understanding. They are perform-ances students can do that show their understanding of a text. Students must understand a text to do any of the following: argue, debate, apply, explain, connect, organize, exemplify, defend, enact, conclude, or transform ideas. When we post a mastery goal, it contains one of these words such as *explain*, *connect*, or *debate*. For example, in English, we post as a goal for the day to "Identify an example of irony in our short story of X and *explain* how the author uses irony to accomplish a major literary purpose." If students can succeed in this, they have understood the author's craft of irony and one theme in this piece of literature.

But such a goal cannot be isolated. We embed it in a much bigger pic-ture. That broader picture encompasses what this story is about, how it relates to other stories, or how the stories relate to us as individuals or as a group today. Beyond this contextualizing, we think in simple terms about how authors use techniques to impact the reader's thoughts and feelings. The "big picture" gives meaning. It enables students to make links between their experiences and what they already know. So, we have broad, long-term, general goals that set up a month-long unit. We also present more focused, short-term goals for one to two days. "Short-term goals can raise self-efficacy simply by making a task appear more manageable, and they can also enhance perceptions of competence by giving continual feedback that con-veys a sense of mastery" (Stipek, 2002, p. 100).

Short-term goals are steps necessary for completion of the long-term goal or assignment. The short-term and long-term goals can be mastery goals. We expect students to understand the theme of oppression in a full novel as a long-term goal. We expect students to comprehend the oppression of one character in one scene as a short-term mastery goal.

In the Spanish classes taught by a colleague, we noticed the curricular goals posted on the wall. At the beginning of the year, she consults the dis-trict curriculum and writes every skill or understanding that the district sets for that class on a large poster. She then uses a magnetic arrow to point to the curricular goal the class is working on. Sometimes the arrow will stay at one goal for a few days, and sometimes it will rest at one goal for a month; however, the students know what they should achieve for the semester right from the start. Each day, she writes the agenda on the board and links the day's activities to the overarching goal indicated by the arrow on the poster. Completing the tasks set forth on the day's agenda is a proximal or short-term goal. Every student has a shot at completing at least the daily objective on the road to mastering the content set out by the curriculum.

Internet resources are rich opportunities for attaining mastery goals. If a conceptual space is drawn up for students, they can pursue it electronically. For example, with students, the teacher can construct a concept map of a topic in the classroom. Then, students add flesh to the skeleton through Internet search and retrieval. Suppose a domain of inquiry is established in English, such as the historical context of the Western movement as a basis for understanding John Steinbeck's novels. Students can select a subtopic, learn about it through Internet resources, and bring the knowledge to a whole class synthesis. Such Internet searches are constrained by the conceptual space. They are neither prescribed ("Find the birth date of this explorer") nor undirected ("Learn about the Wild West").

Making Tasks Relevant

A mastery goal structure in the classroom does not benefit the students if they do not perceive that the teacher's actions, instructions, and evaluations are relevant. Assor, Kaplan, and Roth (2002) studied teacher behaviors that students associated with engagement in schoolwork. Students reported that "fostering relevance" was one of the most motivating teacher actions. Why should students engage in tasks that are of no relevance, use, or benefit to them? As teachers, we hope that none of the tasks we require of our students is meaningless. Students in secondary school do not want to feel they are being forced to complete worthless reading activities. In fact, studies show that forced, meaningless activity leads to anxiety and anger, which are obviously disengaging.

Researchers use *relevance* to refer to the extent to which the content of instruction is linked to students' direct or recalled experience. One procedure for linking reading to an immediate experience is to provide a hands-on activity such as science inquiry. For example, observational activities in science inquiry may include collecting data and sorting artifacts. Texts associated with these experiences are motivating because they are viewed as relevant and interesting (Guthrie, Wigfield et al., 2006). The students are then motivated to use the text to further explore the subject of inquiry. When teachers connect classroom lessons to "real life" outside the classroom, students report that the lessons seem purposeful and interesting (Assor et al., 2002).

Examples of the benefits of relevance abound in the professional journals. For example, "Motivating Students to Read Physics Content" is an article that focuses on using trade books to motivate students to read within the science classroom (Sprague & Cotturone, 2003). The classroom teacher in the article was frustrated by her students' lack of motivation and effort when asked to read their textbook. Even more to her dismay was their lack of ability to summarize the technical passages. First, she tried using different strategies like "chunking" the reading and using graphic organizers. When this did not work, the teacher showed the movie *Star Wars* to increase student interest based on a sense of relevance. Then she had the students read a small portion of the book *The Science of Star Wars* by Cavelos. It dealt with the physics aspects that she wanted to convey to her students. The reading prompted myriad questions that fueled an enthusiastic dialogue about quantum physics. After the discussion, the teacher offered the students extra credit if they read a chapter or two in the book and wrote a minimum one-page essay describing what they read. The teacher's goal was to have them summarize technical material. Student response was overwhelming; nearly all of the students did the assignment. Students' motivation for reading was boosted by the connection of the book to their recent, vivid experience of seeing the movie. The text had a context.

Equally challenging is the subject matter of chemistry. "What is the relation of the periodic table to our lives?" adolescents ask. A high school science teacher, Allison, shared this example:

At the beginning of the unit on chemistry, my students read articles that explain the basic chemistry behind household items such as perfumes, cosmetics, medicine, household cleaners, and even toothpaste. I find these articles on the Internet from sites that create the products like Cover Girl, or many other Web sites. The students read one article of their choice, and then write a brief summary of the passage as it relates to chemistry. The purpose of this activity is to create a sense of relevance about chemistry by having the students investigate how chemistry affects our everyday lives. I have used this activity with textbook readings, but found that the readings are harder to read and are more abstract. Most of my students have high self-efficacy toward reading Internet articles because they are reading online articles at home on their own computer. The articles discuss relatable objects from their everyday lives. For example, interested students can read an article about the chemistry that is involved in making perfumes and link chemistry to the product. Although the textbook discusses the chemistry of polymers, which are in plastics, many students are not as interested in the polymer passages because they do not know what polymers are and how they relate to their lives.

Using Hands-On Activities

In a survey of middle school teachers, the most frequently recommended activity for motivation was using hands-on activities (Zahorik, 1996). Many teachers use hands-on activities to build a sense of "here and now." Such sensory actions and perceptions enable students to personalize the topic of a reading activity. It is known that the stimulating tasks of directly observing, manipulating, and interacting with something make it meaningful. For instance, in inquiry science, students observe predatory bugs attacking fish in an aquarium or collect data on the health of a stream (e.g., ph or nitrate factors) in their neighborhood. Then, texts on these topics spring to life. A real-world connection is irreplaceable as a source of meaning. With no discernable link to the perceived world around them, adolescents find that long, abstract texts are not only meaningless, but are also aversive and painful to cope with.

One of our colleagues, David, creates a common experience for his 10th-grade English class before reading. This gives a unifying piece of background knowledge that can be used to launch an understanding of the text. During a study of the memoir *Night* by Elie Wiesel, there is a scene in which the Jewish people of Poland are being relocated to Auschwitz in a cattle car. It is important to recognize the significance of this scene because it is the very first in a long series of dehumanizing experiences the author endures. After a few failed efforts, he realized that this scene was difficult for his on-grade level readers to appreciate because they did not know what a cattle car was, and in fact, many did not know what cattle were. Now, before reading this chapter of the book in class, he begins class by placing a duct-tape square on the floor. The square is approximately one-fourth the size of a cattle car. As a warm-up, he asks all the students to stand inside the square. This unfailingly provides four to five minutes of joking, uncomfortable squishing, and wisecracks. When the joke wears off, however, the students face a similar situation to that of the prisoners. He explains that although they are uncomfortable after only five minutes, the prisoners in the chapter they will read today had to stand that way for three days. This activity enables the students to have a slightly more realistic understanding of what the Jewish prisoners encountered. Approaching the book with a much more serious outlook, students understand the chapter a bit better. They have formed mastery goals of wanting to grasp the full story and of seeking to explain how victims suffered.

In our English classes, the lower achieving students often read superficially. Rarely are they motivated to dig deeper. To work with these students, we have them enact a short portion of a section of literature. If we are reading a novel with interaction among characters, we select about three pages and have the students write a play that depicts the meaning of those pages. By composing and practicing the parts, they read between the lines, imagine the characters' feelings, and link the portion to prior sections. In short, knowing they have to act it out motivates them to deeply understand it. When this understanding dawns on students, their interest grows. As the text makes sense, they move forward with more confidence and eagerness. A brief experience of nuanced meaning sets the standard for their understanding of the next portion.

Mastery Versus Performance Motivation: Theory and Research

Mastery goals describe the motivation of students who want to understand or develop skills. Students are motivated to master the material because it is relevant or interesting. The "opposing" goal structure is referred to as performance-goal structure. Performance-goal-oriented students generally want to "get the best grade" and be academically superior to their peers (Stipek, 2002). One might ask, "What is the problem with encouraging students to get high grades?" The problem with performance goals is that "while . . . performance goals may actually lend themselves to successful academic performance in the short term . . . they do not lend themselves to the types of . . . learning characteristics associated with self-regulated learning" (Nichols, Jones, & Hancock, 2003, p. 77).

With performance goals, students seek to meet the external demand of finishing assignments, completing homework, or getting every item right on the test. Not being concerned with deep understanding, these students use superficial strategies such as memorizing and question answering without deep understanding. Superficial strategies lead to minimal comprehension, however, and long-term knowledge development suffers. Moreover, students do not gain the stronger strategies for reading harder, more complex, more advanced text (Pintrich, 2000). Driven only by performance goals, students do not prepare themselves for future schooling.

Another drawback of performance goals, even performance approach goals ("I want to get the highest grade"), is that they do not require students to be involved in what they are learning. Students who study and write only for the "A" miss out on the joy of learning. According to the study performed by Nichols, Jones, and Hancock (2003), teachers who promoted performance goals had students who reported high levels of boredom, a lack of joy, and disinterest in their daily lessons. Students need to feel that what they are learning and reading is relevant and important. In a classroom where mastery is the emphasis, the goal is for students to be involved in their own learning and understanding.

That being said, performance goals can be positive indicators of achievement. When students use performance goals to approach the material with a competitive attitude, called approach performance goals, students can actually achieve quite well (Nichols et al., 2003). Teachers often witness this phenomenon. We recognize the student who comes into the classroom with the confidence that he can and will get an A in this class. He studies and works hard to ensure that the A is his. It is ideal for students to have performance approach goals ("I want the highest possible grade") combined with the mastery goals ("I really want to understand this material"). These students achieve the greatest success in secondary school. Grades are here to stay, and comprehending fully is invaluable; effective teachers urge students toward both.

The threat to achievement arises when students have no other aims beyond the performance goals. When performance-oriented students fail, they may adopt self-handicapping strategies. They purposefully create an excuse for failure, such as not studying, procrastinating, or drinking heavily the night before an exam. This prevents failure from undermining their sense of worth (Covington, 2000). Unfortunately, students who cope with their fear of failure to get good grades by handicapping themselves usually sabotage their own chances at success (Urdan, 2004).

While performance goals can lead to achievement, it is important that students recognize the role that effort plays in their successes or failures. Teachers who adopt a mastery approach to their teaching enable students to attribute success to effort instead of innate ability. More important, when teachers inspire mastery goal setting in their students, students will attribute failures to lack of engagement in class activities such as reading, instead of lack of ability or self-worth. Thus, they usually persevere in the face of difficulty (Weiner, 1994). If students view engagement in literature as part of the effort put into success, they will be more motivated to read with a purpose.

Transforming Text to Meaning

In a 10th-grade, on-grade level English class, we have struggled to refine the way we include note taking to help students gain the gratification of deeper understanding. Note taking is a familiar enterprise to students by the time they reach their sophomore year in high school. As such, we often have been guilty of employing it simply to manage the classroom. With modifications, however, it offers an opportunity of opening up all texts to student interest and involvement. We have utilized note taking with a subject journal in a unit of study for William Golding's *Lord of the Flies*. The namesake symbol of the novel is a pig's head that has been severed and left in the jungle as a sacrificial offering to the potential for evil that resides in each human's heart. This is an abstract concept even for adults to grasp, leaving many sophomores befuddled. Our approach to this aspect of the novel is to discuss the theme of humanity's evil before beginning a reading of the book.

Earlier in the curriculum, the students have read works such as *Night* by Elie Wiesel and *The Odyssey* by Homer, so we use these works and their themes as groundwork. Once students have identified the emotional responses to anger and rage and how the desire to fulfill impulses can arise in all humans, we ask the students to keep a journal during our reading of *Lord of the Flies*. The students know what they are looking for, only because they are forced to reflect on their own experiences. Strictly observing the traits of the text does not promote enough of a mental exchange to consistently develop meaning and comprehension. We inform the students that as the novel progresses they will find more instances of the thoughts, words, and actions of the characters that are more representative of evil and selfishness. They then find these examples and reflect on them in their journals. We have found the journal to be very successful in building personal connections to the novel through which students have strong reactions to particular characters based on their identity.

Limitations, no doubt, exist for this attempt to motivate. Some students in the class will simply refuse to work on a cumbersome note taking journal assignment. Often, significant issues with vocabulary, jargon, dialect, or decoding prevent enough information from being gleaned. Giving the students a simple focus and an opportunity to contribute their own experiences to a text, however, allows for a deeper understanding, and possibly more important, a deeper enjoyment.

This is an example of transforming text to meaning. As a collection of thoughts, opinions, reactions, feelings, and even confusions, the journal is a gallery of personal meanings. Certainly, some specific entries are more "accurate" representations of the text than others are—comprehension is seldom "perfect." But the process of reading to react, and recording one's views, is transforming. It places the text into a new relationship to oneself. Both the material and the person take on a slightly new shape with this transformation. The process of transforming begins with the background knowledge, values, and emotions of the reader. Confronting the novelty in the text, the reader blends the new text and the old views and understandings. Readers create something very new and unique, a meaning distinctive to themselves, or at least partially so.

When students transform, they leap away from boredom. A meaningless text is inevitably boring because the student cannot connect to it. Without meaning, the text cannot be happy, sad, rich, poor, inspiring, or learnable. It is dead. Such deadness is disengaging, which leads to an avoidance rather than the embrace of reading (Seifert & O'Keefe, 2001). Transformation of text reflects a type of learning that rewards student effort. Learning at this level satisfies the need for competence, which all individuals, especially students as readers, possess (Ryan & Deci, 2000a). When students build personal meaning from text, they are inherently gratified because they know they have been competent in their encounter.

Countless types of transformations can be found in mastery-oriented classrooms. These include those in the following table.

Table 2.1   Transformations

Existing Text—In Curriculum	Transformed Text—From Student
Page on life cycles in life science textbook	Diagram of the life cycle of a butterfly
Time warp in a literary story	Chronological time line for story
Military build up in historical text	Same time period from economic perspective
Drama in English	Short narrative from one character's view
Math formula	Written explanation of formula
Word problem in math	Diagram of problem
Any linear text	Concept map with spatial layout
Long text of five pages	Short text of ten sentences
Short text of ten sentences	Long text of five pages

In composing transformations, we give students choice. For example, in English, we ask students whether they prefer to write a poem or personal narrative to show the meanings in the first portion of a novel in our curriculum. We may ask partners to share and explain their transformation with a classmate. We may ask students to post them or show them on an overhead. Then the class points out what the transformation showed that the original text did not. Students realize the power of their transformations when they see them help others. The motivation that goes into composing a compelling transformation is contagious.

Scaffolding Mastery Motivation

Mastery goals can induce fear. They seem abstract and hard to accomplish. Scaffolding will take all of the guesswork (and a lot of the anxiety) out of being a student in your class. The idea behind a mastery goal structure is understanding and skill building; it is not a competition between students to see who can best guess what the exam will cover or what exactly the teacher had in mind when assigning the essay. Before assigning tasks, we provide rubrics for the mastery goal. The rubric is a set of performances from low level to high level that shows different degrees of competency. For the goal of "understanding oppression" in a novel, an example of a simplified rubric follows: State the plot and roles of main characters (one point), state the relationship of two characters (two points), explain how one character is oppressing another character or group (three points), and elaborate the many forms and sources of oppression in the novel (four points). Lower levels (one to two) show simple comprehension. Higher levels (three to four) illustrate deeper comprehension of the novel and its theme.

To help students attain higher levels, we discuss the skills they will need to demonstrate to do well on the assignment. Then, we model the skills necessary for completing the assignment well, letting them practice this skill. Students watch and coach one another. We provide feedback along the way, indicating their progress or other strategies they might employ in developing this skill. Finally, we show samples of completed versions of the assignment. As a class, we discuss the evaluation of several anonymous samples of students' work, using the scoring guide that is connected to the rubric.

This suggestion not only makes the goal of the assignment clear (by providing rubrics, evaluating examples, and modeling the skills), but also demonstrates to students that the task is challenging but attainable. If a teacher assigns a worksheet during class that does not require much thought or complex ideas, students call it "busy work." If you have ever been assigned busy work, you know how disengaging it can be. Work that does not require much thought may be easier, and even preferable if assigned a grade strictly for correct answers. But students often feel more reward when completing challenging tasks because they are more engaging (Brophy & Alleman, 1991). When teachers provide attainable yet challenging texts, students are not bored by them.

Since we are creating challenging goals for our students' reading, we provide them with models, samples, and plenty of opportunities to practice. This allows them to feel confident in their reading skills. In a math study, students reported preferring the math classes in which they thought that both the challenge level and their confidence in their ability to complete the classwork were high (Turner et al., 1998). Without providing the scaffolding for success at challenging tasks, students will become anxious about the material instead of feeling confident.

Teachers may shy away from scaffolding, claiming that it "gives away the answers," but let us provide an example of what we mean. One of the 10th-grade goals for reading *The Taming of the Shrew* is to understand how Shakespeare creates humor in the play. After discussing and identifying comedic devices, we introduce the assignment that will evaluate their mastery of this understanding: a page-long response identifying a 40- to 50-line passage from the play that explains how Shakespeare creates humor in that passage. We start with the rubric. Since *The Taming of the Shrew* is the last work we read for the semester, and since we have used the same rubric for every page-long response, the review of the rubric is brief. The first time, however, we examine each component of the rubric and exactly what we are looking for when we evaluate each requirement. Then we point students to a 45-line passage, distribute copies they can annotate, and put a copy on the overhead so they can follow along. Together, we find examples of comedic devices, noting in the margins of the projected copy the students' explanations of how each example creates humor or why it is funny. In this way, we model how to write an explanation for the way the device works within the text.

Finally, we distribute samples of responses to that passage. As a class, we use the rubric to evaluate each. If left at that, we would consider this method "giving away the answers," but the students must choose a different passage and write a brief constructed response (BCR) showing their engagement with and understanding of the text. At this point, they understand the objective of the response, they have practiced the reading skill, and they are mastery learners in this situation.

Providing Reteach Opportunities

We employ a reteach policy. Its point is to offer multiple opportunities for students to demonstrate mastery of learning goals. Reteaching occurs when teachers or students determine that students are not meeting learning goals. The teacher determines the method and schedule for reteaching. He also determines the assignments that are "reassessable" ahead of time and lets the students know when these opportunities are available. Students have one opportunity to reassess for a grade. The idea is that some students take more time and practice to achieve mastery of a learning goal. These students, then, receive an opportunity to attend a reteach session with the teacher to get more practice and instruction before their reassessment. The reassessed grade is the final grade. If the student or teacher feels that more practice and instruction are needed, the teacher can certainly offer more reteaching, but the student only gets one reassessment opportunity. The teacher decides the nature and time of the reteaching session, but students must attend to be eligible for reassessment.

When reassessing students, we give them the same task based on a new reading. For example, if we asked students to write a BCR contrasting the tones of two poems after teaching the class about tone through various methods and some students do not demonstrate a mastery of the identification and explanation of tone using textual support, we suggest that they come to a reteach session on tone. If the students take this opportunity, they will be reassessed by writing a BCR contrasting the tones of two new poems. This practice prevents students from simply editing based on teacher feedback and requires them to demonstrate their knowledge of the mastery objective, using textual evidence to identify and explain the creation of tone in two poems.

This policy has many positive effects on our students' motivation, such as mastery-goal orientation, attributing success to effort, and increased self-efficacy. The policy also promotes students' confidence in us as their educators. It sends the message that we know they can learn the material, and we will work hard with them to reach their mastery goals.

As educators, our paramount goal is for our students to learn, not earn a grade. A mastery-oriented classroom is a better learning environment because it promotes learning. The reteach and reassess policy fosters mastery goals in the classroom and task involvement in our students. For example, if a student does not meet standards for mastery on an assignment designed to measure a certain level of engagement with the literature, he has a chance to relearn it, and we have a chance to reteach it.

Emphasizing mastery, instead of a grade, promotes mastery orientation. We have many students who are still concerned only with the grade when they come to the reteach session, but this time they are determined to understand the processes of learning this material. Since the reassessment consists of a new text, they must learn the skill to apply it to the unfamiliar text. Regurgitating class discussion does not show mastery, and this performance-goal approach to the assignment will not work for them on the reassessment. Performance-oriented students are almost forced to be task involved when taking advantage of the reteach and reassess policy.

The reteach and reassess policy creates an environment of learning that promotes effort and persistence. Giving students the opportunity to master a skill over time and with repeated attempts may change their ideas about how and why they succeed in class. If we offer our students the opportunity to try again, and really work with them to achieve, perhaps their perceptions of the causes of achievement can change from an innate ability to perform to persistence and effort.

The reteach and reassess policy assures that students will learn. If a student did not learn the material as it was taught to the rest of the class, ideally, he has a second chance to relearn it at his own pace or in his own way. The idea of a "second chance" emphasizes the importance of learning a task and promotes a mastery goal, creating an environment where students feel confident in their teacher to make the task meaningful and, thus, motivating.

Rewarding Effort Over Performance

Trying to understand high school text is tough work. Student effort is imperative. How do we help students generate that effort? In his review of the research literature concerning "Goal Theory, Motivation, and School," Covington (2000) insisted that "mastery-oriented students tend to believe that effort is the key to success, and that failure, despite trying hard, does not necessarily imply incompetence, but simply not having employed the right learning strategies" (p. 175). When providing feedback, attribute successes to effort or the use of an effective strategy. Attribute failures to lack of effort or the implementation of an ineffective strategy.

Students will often create their own attributions for the grades they get, such as, "She hates me" or "I'm stupid," but take the time to force the students to reflect on effort attributional feedback you provide on their work. Most students look for the grade first, and then read the feedback if it is available. If the grade is poor, students are less likely to read the feedback, which is counterproductive. Last semester, we received phone calls from a student's parents who were not accustomed to their child receiving B's and C's on essays. "He usually gets A's on writing assignments," they remarked. At the parent conference, we presented the student's portfolio of work. The same comments were on every assignment. The student, who was also present at the conference, suddenly realized why he was receiving poor grades on his writing. He had never bothered to apply the feedback to his next assignment. To him, all that mattered was the grade. He looked at that and got discouraged with the class and his ability to engage in and write about the text. If it is the grade in which students show interest, make reflections part of an assignment grade. When we return essays to our students, we make them answer two questions about their writing in hopes that they will learn from their mistakes. We develop these questions based on the most common errors found during our grading.

In a review of the research, Schunk (2003) concluded that providing feedback based on effort ("You didn't do well because you didn't work hard enough") encourages mastery goal orientation and continued effort through failures. Schunk also pointed out, however, that effort can only take students so far. As students continue to try and fail, they must receive feedback that will direct them to new strategies. Feedback needs to reflect students' efforts and use of learning strategies, including reading. If students do particularly well on a task, remind them that reading material helped them with this achievement. If they are not performing well, students must use their reading strategies to understand the text, assignment, or main ideas.

As noted by Schunk (2003), when students develop the skills necessary to complete a task, comments such as, "You've been working hard," are less likely to motivate. Over time, similar tasks should become easier; if they are not, then the students need feedback that provides new strategies for success. A study of undergraduate students by Church, Elliot, and Gable (2001) found that harsh evaluation not only compelled students to adopt performance-avoidance goals, but also prevented them from adopting mastery goals. The study asked students to rate the truth of statements such as, "The grading structure makes it almost impossible to get an A in this course," or "High grades are seldom obtained by students in this course." Research suggests that extremely high standards for performance are not indicators of rigor, but instead may generate a performance orientation among students.

Rubric writing may be reevaluated in the light of reducing harsh evaluation. Rubrics that we use to evaluate student writing or performance are generic in nature and include skills that we have modeled and that the students have practiced. Each section of the rubric has a scale from one to six. The students know that a five or six is an A grade, four is in B territory, three looks like a C, two a D, and one an F. To do poorly, students have to really ignore several sections of the rubric. There are many opportunities for an A grade in that points are not awarded for specific areas of the rubric, just for the completion of general skill areas. Students who really want to impress the teacher and work toward a six in all areas can certainly do that, but earning all fives also earns students an A grade. Students who want to compare and are performance oriented can still show off their row of sixes, but students who tried hard and used all the skills necessary to complete the task are happy with their A or B. Again, we scaffold mastery motivation by giving rubrics as road maps for success. As students learn to follow these maps, they grow in motivation and engagement for academic reading.

3

Control and Choice

Supporting Self-Directed Reading

Sarah Fillman and John T. Guthrie
University of Maryland

High school English teachers often run into a wall of unmotivated individuals. Many students simply do not want to read. Without our insistence, students are rarely motivated to pick up Homer's *The Odyssey*. Because this text is so archaic, the language, epic conventions, and plot serve as foils to the students' comprehension. They do not read it because they feel incapable of understanding the text, it is not relevant to their lives, and there are no apparent rewards. In the long term, a lack of motivation often leads to behavioral or psychological problems and dropout (Linnenbrink & Pintrich, 2002). Although we put forth our best efforts to motivate these students to read, it seems we simply cannot save them all.

For any single student, there are many sources of low motivation. These include a home environment that does not endorse reading, a history of failures in learning to read, a lack of positive experience with books, and a peer group that shuns school reading. In addition, many students share a common school experience that decreases their reading motivation. All students have moved from the elementary level, where they had a self-contained classroom, a nurturing teacher, and many freedoms. In middle school, the heightened structure includes many different classes, bigger textbooks, daily assignments, large class size, more competition, and teacher control of instruction. Opportunities for students to choose books or to follow their interests drop precipitously. This loss comes just at the age when students are seeking independence and control of their lives. Such a culture shock is typically demotivating (L. H. Anderman & E. M. Anderman, 1999; Wigfield, 2004).

At the same time, middle and high school teachers cannot turn every page for every student. Students must take responsibility and become self-directing, or else they flounder. To direct themselves in middle and high school, students have to *want* to learn from texts. Without this desire, they will simply not do sufficient reading to succeed. This desire cannot be entirely external, derived completely from teachers, parents, or requirements for a class. Students must want to read, write, and learn for themselves. The combination of these internal motivations, along with external ones, is ideal.

A problem arises if a student's motivation is solely external (e.g., grades, points, parent satisfaction). For these students, success is limited. They are likely to do only the assigned work and are not likely to read deeply. They are prone to cutting corners, memorizing for the short term, and reading to score a grade, but not to conquer the content. To succeed in secondary school, students need to become internally motivated. They need to be choosing, deciding, owning, controlling, and taking charge of their reading. Such an internally motivated student soon becomes an achiever (Ryan & Deci, 2000b)

Providing Control and Choice in Instruction

As teachers, we often suppose things are going well when we are leading, students are attentive, and topics are getting covered. Students, however, may see instruction differently. Researchers have discovered from questioning students that many simple teacher actions are actually quite disengaging for students (Assor, Kaplan, & Roth, 2002). For example, students report that the following practices are very demotivating:

- The teacher stops me when I am reading something interesting.
- The teacher tells me what to do all the time.
- The teacher gives me homework that does not help me understand the topic.
- The teacher only listens to people who share her opinions.
- The teacher makes me read boring books.

Many of these teacher actions may seem necessary or perhaps innocent. According to students, however, these actions are disaffecting. In contrast, students report that they are more engaged in classrooms where they experience the following:

- The teacher relates the material to us.
- The teacher listens to all opinions and voices her own opinions as well.
- The teacher sometimes allows us to choose what we learn.
- If we are writing something interesting, we may finish.
- The teacher helps us find our own ways to learn (Assor, Kaplan, & Roth, 2002; Skinner, Wellborn, & Connell, 1990).

Practices like these have high impact on students in a short time-frame. One researcher observed teachers in a brief, 10 minute lesson on how to solve a problem (Reeve & Jang, 2006). Afterward, he asked students about their motivation and their sense of being in charge of their learning in the task. Students were demotivated when the teacher did the following: talked constantly, gave detailed directions, asked controlling questions, gave deadlines, criticized students, and gave answers before students finished.

In contrast, students reported feeling engaged and motivated for the tasks when teachers did the following: listened, asked what students wanted, provided a rationale for work, picked up on student questions, gave encouraging feedback, and recognized challenges.

Of course, teachers must talk and give directions. But the balance of both sets of practices is what counts. Excessive *teacher*-centeredness (e.g., only teacher talk) is more disengaging than we imagine. At the same time, excessive *student*-centeredness (e.g., only student initiative) may be unproductive. Our goal is to move from teacher overcontrol to student empowerment, to right the balance and get a better blend of these actions in our classrooms.

Overview of Instructional Practices

In a perfect world, our students would yearn to learn because they are busy, independent, knowledge-stimulated beings. Instead, we know from experience that even in advanced placement classes, our students often meet us with apathy or resistance. Instead of doing their homework immediately after school, students meet with distractions such as television, video games, cell phone text messaging, and sports. Many parents expect adolescents to find employment, and this necessity may interfere with reading. Motivating the kids that sit in our classrooms today is a tall task. Although there is no magic wand to motivate students, we must try to reach them in hopes of equipping them with the motivation for reading that promotes more and more learning.

We believe there are six practices that realistically cultivate motivation. The first teaching practice is helping students gain *ownership of text*. Students need to believe that they have some control of *what* they read for school. Coupled with this sense of being in charge of what they read, the second practice is giving students *options for how to learn* from their texts. Students need to find their own ways to reach the goals of understanding. Third, we advocate student *input into curriculum*. Much more conservative than it sounds, this simply refers to student choices of subtopics or sequences within a mandated unit of study. Fourth, we provide opportunity for *self-selection of knowledge displays*. Given options of how to show they have understood a text, students are often motivated to read. Fifth, it is very feasible to follow the example of many teachers who give students a *voice in standards for evaluating* their learning from text. Obviously, students do not fully set the standards by which they are judged, but students can have a say in designing scoring guides connected to the rubrics or defining how grades align with the levels. Sixth, in many subjects, teachers share control through *inquiry projects*. Such projects allow for student decision making within a common framework. These all give students a bit of investment in their learning from school text. Along the way, we present evidence that student choices are important for motivation.

Ownership of Text

When we think of giving choices in reading, we imagine students having a decision on *what book* to read. Although not the only choice, it is a starting place. One of our colleagues, middle school English teacher Melissa, always tries to make extra texts available to students. She encourages them to supplement the school-designed curriculum (and teacher-chosen texts) with books they choose. She has seen how the students react to finding a book they enjoy. She has witnessed students who usually come into the classroom saying that they "hate reading" and leave with a list of books they want to read over the summer.

Melissa changed her teaching after reading an article titled, "Exploring Sixth Graders' Selection of Nonfiction Trade Books" (Moss & Hendershot, 2002). These authors note that the reason many middle school children are not reading is not because they do not enjoy reading, but because they do not enjoy reading what the school assigns. Given suitable texts, these students often spend time reading about subjects that interest them, such as history, science, and technology. Moss and Hendershot noted that "by giving students access to this body of literature, teachers may provide middle graders with new ways into literacy and greater motivation for reading" (pp. 7–8). Students developed an internal desire to read when they were able to find things that related to their interests and their lives outside school.

Providing the choice of which book to read is not always possible. Many high school courses are anchored to an adopted textbook. Science and history teachers can seldom neglect the assigned text. Within this situation, many choices are still possible. A teacher rarely assigns all chapters on all topics in a comprehensive text. If some selection is possible or even necessary, students can participate in the decisions. For example, in a science textbook with 10 topics, students can read all, but choose one in which to specialize. Each student reads his specialty deeply, summarizes it, and explains it to the team or class. He takes charge of that topic. He takes "ownership" of the text on that topic; that is his domain. Perhaps he writes one to two questions on his topic as a learning tool for classmates or as a quiz item. Substantial experimental evidence verifies the claim that instruction with embedded choices of books and self-questioning increases students' curiosity and reading achievement, in comparison to traditional reading instruction (Guthrie, Wigfield, & Von Secker, 2000).

Within a textbook, student choices can take many forms. Teachers often ask students to do the following: (1) find one example of irony in a poem, (2) locate one fair-minded general in this war, (3) identify one animal in the biology book that shows a mutualism with ants, and (4) show how two people can say the same thing in different ways in this (foreign) language. Each activity is a microchoice. Teachers who foster ownership give many microchoices every class period. Students in these classrooms show interest and engagement. Many teachers, however, give few choices or none at all. Students in these confining environments often feel controlled, and some individuals become alienated. Many students in overly controlling classrooms disengage, do not read, or muddle through, at best (Assor et al., 2002).

To help students become choosers, effective teachers give students as much self-direction as they can handle. For advanced students, a wide spectrum of reading choices is possible and productive. For on-grade level readers, we reduce the menu but still give some options of which text to read. For below-grade level readers, we usually give microchoices within a text that we have selected to match their reading level. For this group, selecting which section, page, paragraph, or caption may be the level of choice they can manage at a certain time. Our goal is to meet learners where they are as owners of reading, and then move slowly up the ladder toward fuller independence.

Options for How to Learn From Text

Most high school teachers give choices for *how* to learn from text. Across many content areas, teachers suggest that students take notes or write a summary. Some teachers recommend that students write questions and then answer them. Other teachers encourage making an outline or a concept map as a spatial organization of the text. For some teachers, all of these options are acceptable. If a teacher explains (or better yet, teaches) these different reading strategies and allows students to hand them in for a grade, she has offered options for how to learn from text.

Melissa's Grade 7 classes must follow the county curriculum that dictates the texts students should read and the final projects that all students in the county must complete. For each unit, the students write an essay analyzing one aspect of the book: character development, setting, or plot structure. In the first unit, she guided the reading with questions focusing on character development to help students organize their ideas prior to writing their essay. With little opportunity to direct their own learning, students displayed low ownership of their learning and no self-discovery. Their writing exhibited a low level of understanding.

In the second unit, Melissa created more opportunities for students to have increased self-direction in preparing for the essays. She defined their final goal as an essay about the setting. She allowed them to choose the book they would read (from a list of approved county books). Then, she challenged them to display the setting of their book to the class. Students chose to write a descriptive paragraph, draw an illustration, or create a shadow box, and some even brought in materials to re-create the setting in the classroom. The students developed a much deeper level of understanding when they self-directed than they did when they used teacher-directed materials, and their essays were much richer and deeper as a result.

In the third unit, Melissa was even more open about the prewriting activities. She found, however, that the students needed some teacher direction to stay on track and feel like they understood what they were doing. Melissa began this third unit giving the students too much freedom of choice. Because she did not provide suggested ideas for presentation, many students felt overwhelmed and stressed about the project. Finding the right balance of teacher-directed and student-directed learning is a challenge. Nevertheless, when the balance is struck, students show inspiring levels of understanding and greater motivation.

Another colleague, Mark, found his math students to be notoriously unmotivated to read word problems. They did not complete homework assignments on word problems, even when he assigned the "first half only" on a particular page. To motivate his students, he gave them the option of completing the odd items or the even items in the back of one chapter (both covered the same principle). Mark could not believe the result; 90% of the students completed the homework. Remarkably, many students read all of the problems to decide which ones were the easiest. Then, after doing them all, they handed in the half on which they thought they did best. Sometimes the smallest option for how to learn gives students the investment they need to engage with text.

Input Into Curriculum

A vast majority of states, counties, and schools fully spell out their curricula. Often, teachers are accountable for students' test scores on a network of objectives in English, science, history, foreign language, or math. Even so, teachers decide daily about which topic to emphasize, which skill to promote, or which objective to give the most weight. In this selection process, students can participate. Teachers who emphasize motivation ask students their opinions, poll for preferences, hold a vote, or give students input within a limited scope.

Recently, we compared two 10th-grade honors classes; in one class, we assigned the topics for a debate, and in the other, we gave a choice from a menu of topics for the debate. We discovered a huge difference in motivation, engagement, and overall student success. When we arbitrarily assigned the topics to students, the debate, though supported by textual quotes, was somewhat dry and uninteresting. Many students spoke only one or two times during the debate, receiving a low score for participation. The students who chose their topic, however, not only seemed more engaged in the preparation of their debate (e.g., finding quotes from George Orwell's *1984,* as well as current articles that supported their argument), but also delivered their arguments with more fervor and with a multitude of quotes from outside sources. Astounded by the amount of preparation that went into the debate involving choice, we concluded that when giving a debate assignment, students must be able to select a topic of personal interest. As teachers, we have perceived that students who are interested in the material are more motivated to prepare for and complete an assignment.

All content areas provide opportunities to use choice. Shana is a science teacher who often incorporates choice into her science lessons. She commented, "My colleagues and I use choice constantly. In the science curriculum, we are always trying to incorporate inquiry into daily practices." In addition, she said, "Inquiry requires student choice; students must be able to choose the angle of their exploration to develop their own testable questions." Although she often uses choice to aid in classroom management,

Shana claimed that choice is needed to motivate students to make appropriate behavioral decisions.

Student Self-Direction and Shared Control: Theory and Research

Two elements of a classroom, student self-direction and shared control, exist in a spiral. When teachers provide a class some opportunity to contribute to content and the management of a particular course, they are sharing control. Within this context for learning, many students become more self-directing by participating more fully and taking responsibility for their work. They become more motivationally and cognitively engaged in the reading for this course. Note that this enhanced engagement many not extend to other courses, other teachers, or books in other subjects. In parallel, when students begin a course, or when they come to class in a state of self-direction, they show interest, preparation, and commitment to the learning activities. For these students (or perhaps, for a full class of them), teachers provide broader opportunities for independent work. That is, teachers share control with students who present themselves as engaged in the course. Thus, a positive spiral turns upward during the year (Skinner & Belmont, 1993). This occurs in elementary school as well as middle school or high school (Deci & Ryan, 2000; Lepola, 2004; Lepola, Salonen, & Vauras, 2004; Stipek, 2002).

Simultaneously, the spiral can be negative. If teachers are overcontrolling, students disengage. When teachers are too directive, too insistent on micromanagement, or too teacher-centered, students retreat into passivity or avoidance. Students do assignments only reluctantly, if at all, and they read as little as possible (Ivey, 2002). Likewise, teachers usually react to disengaged students by becoming more controlling. For example, when students refuse to read for homework, teachers give tests over homework reading. Not wanting to fail, students read, but reluctantly. They read because they are coerced, not because they are interested. The result is a test score, but not deep knowledge growth or topic interest (Assor et al., 2002). In this way, the sword of shared control cuts both ways, toward building and demolishing student engagement.

Because many teachers embrace a relatively controlling classroom climate, many classes do not offer students much choice in what and how they learn. School policies and rules largely influence teachers, who often implement strategies because of external pressures such as school regulations and state tests. For many teachers, "the concept of autonomy is an unfamiliar—even foreign—concept" (Reeve, Jang, Carrell, Jeon, & Barch, 2004, p. 149).

Studies suggest, however, that when teachers incorporate more choice and autonomy-supportive strategies into teaching practices and "find ways to involve and satisfy their students' psychological needs (for autonomy, competence, and relatedness)" (p. 149), students show greater motivation. Based on questionnaires given to teachers and students, students are more likely to be internally motivated when teachers share control and support students' interests than they are when teachers overdirect the classroom (Reeve et al., 2004; Reeve & Jang, 2006; Skinner & Belmont, 1993).

To discover more about providing student choices, researchers Flowerday and Schraw (2000) interviewed secondary teachers to find out what kinds of choices they actually give in the classroom. Teachers reported that they focused on the following: (1) topic of study, (2) reading materials, (3) methods of assessment, (4) order of activities, (5) social arrangements, and (6) procedural choices. Most choices focused on topic of study or reading materials, since teachers are required to conduct certain types of assessments and because many students lack the knowledge of what types of things should be assessed. Teachers concluded, however, that "some choice of assessment greatly enhanced a student's sense of autonomy and personal control" (Flowerday & Schraw, 2000, p. 634). Teachers said that their purposes were to increase student self-determination and personal interest. They believed that all grades should use choice, with older students needing more choices as student competence and self-regulation increase.

Every teacher has his own style, making each classroom unique. However, some parts of a teacher's approach are more motivating than others. Assor et al. (2002) conducted a study to determine whether students could differentiate among various types of autonomy-enhancing and teacher-suppressing behaviors in a typical classroom. The authors concluded that adolescents can distinguish between the various teacher behaviors that do and do not give them more control over a situation. In controlled experiments, when investigators gave students a choice that allowed them to select tasks that were interesting to them (intrinsic frame), students felt in control of their work. On the other hand, when investigators gave students the goal of trying to meet an external standard (extrinsic frame), students thought they were being manipulated by an outsider. With the intrinsic frame, students read more conceptually; with the extrinsic frame, students read more superficially (Vansteenkiste, Simons, Lens, Soenens, & Matos, 2005). When students feel that teachers support their autonomy, they are apt to value the task and experience positive feelings toward it, which impacts positively on their achievement (Grolnick, Ryan, & Deci, 1991).

It is also often problematic to provide reading choices because many teachers are forced to use the textbook or have limited resources to provide for their students. Good starting points, however, include: (1) offering simple choices at first, (2) helping students practice making good choices, (3) providing feedback about their choices, (4) using team choices for younger students, (5) offering information that clarifies the choice, and (6) affording choices within a task (e.g., ordering, sequence, topic). This is similar to scaffolding for a cognitive skill like drawing conclusions. Teachers initially share responsibility with students for their choices. Gradually, teachers shift decision making to students.

Professional development is profitable for teachers who are in the process of becoming more autonomy-supportive. In one study, a professor conducted an informational session with 20 high school teachers on how to support students' autonomy. Teachers learned to use a Web site that gave examples and further explanations for these techniques. After teachers returned to the classroom, observers rated them on their levels of autonomy support. Observers also determined the students' engagement based on their active task involvement during instruction. Teachers who went through the training used more autonomy-supportive behaviors than other teachers. Their actions in the classroom raised the engagement level of their students (Reeve et al., 2004).

Of course, educators are accountable for test scores in reading. Importantly, many studies report that reading comprehension test scores positively correlate with intrinsic motivation for reading. A. W. Gottfried, Cook, and A. E. Gottfried (2005) showed that students with exceptionally high academic, intrinsic motivation outperformed other students on various reading measures from the elementary through the high school grades. In a sample of high school students, Schiefele (1996) found that interest correlated with text learning when other factors such as text length, text genre, method of learning the text (e.g., recognition vs. recall), background knowledge, and age or grade level were controlled. Personal interest correlated more highly with deep-level learning than with surface-level learning from texts (Schiefele, 1996; Schiefele & Krapp, 1996). Furthermore, the correlation of intrinsic motivation and achievement has been shown for a variety of reading comprehension measures including standardized tests such as the Woodcock-Johnson (A. E. Gottfried, 1990), the IEA Literacy Test (Wang & Guthrie, 2004), the Metropolitan Achievement Test Comprehension Measure (Guthrie, Wigfield, & Von Secker, 2000), and others (Lepola, 2004). Reading grades have been used extensively in this literature as well (A. E. Gottfried, 1990; Sweet, Guthrie, & Ng, 1998; Wang & Guthrie, 2004). Finally, students' perceived control and choice are associated positively with achievement in reading (Skinner, Wellborn, & Connell, 1990; Sweet, Guthrie, & Ng, 1998).

Self-Selection of Knowledge Displays

Creative teachers often find ways to allow students a fraction of freedom in showing what they have learned from reading. Suppose a teacher taught a fundamental principle, formula, technique, relationship, or concept in a subject. For a teacher, a student's choice of the particular content for displaying knowledge is less important than whether she got the main point. For example, in English, students can display their understanding of a novel's theme by conveying it from the perspective of one of several characters. If students choose the character in such an evaluation, they will write with more elaboration than they will if the teacher chooses the same character for all to write about. In a biology lab test of the procedures for measuring the chemical "pollution" of water, students can select from three levels of clear to polluted water for the test, all of which show their level of expertise. These instructional practices increase students' commitment to reading by increasing their estimation of the value of these literacy tasks (Thorkildsen, 2002).

To illustrate the use of choice in evaluation, we recount how our 12th-grade classes chose their final assessment for Tom Stoppard's play *Rosencrantz and Guildenstern Are Dead.* The topic of study had already been determined, though many of the students suggested that we not teach the same play in the future because of its complexities. Taking that into consideration, as a class, we brainstormed different types of assessments that could be used for this play other than the traditional end-of-the-book test. We came up with two alternate forms of assessments that would be an equal replacement of a unit test. Option one consisted of creating a poster displaying a list of characters with descriptions and quotes from the play for each, the re-creation of two scenes using pictures (either hand drawn or from magazines or the Internet), some element of the Theatre of the Absurd (the genre to which the play belongs), and a list of vocabulary and definitions used in the play.

Option two was constructing an exam consisting of questions based on the play, literary techniques, and the Theatre of the Absurd elements. Students had to write five true/false questions, five multiple-choice questions, and three essay questions. For this option, students provided an answer key for the objective section and a thesis for each of the essay questions. The class brainstormed the steps of the assessment choices for 20 minutes. We were able to monitor the students' choices to ensure that the assessment options were appropriate for evaluating student knowledge.

Choice in this final assessment proved successful. Students worked in pairs, and for the most part, the success rate was high. Students demonstrated their understanding of the play in various ways, and because they chose the form of assessment, the process by which they completed the assignment, and who they worked with, they were more successful than if we had created a unit test. In the end, because the students had choices, they felt more enthusiastic about either crafting a poster that displayed their abilities or creating a test that demonstrated their knowledge. Because of our success in offering choice to students, we continue to offer choice in gradual increments, scaffolding appropriate choices to help them complete learning tasks. This requires feedback during group brainstorming activities, as well as feedback on chosen assignments (Lutz, Guthrie, & Davis, 2006).

Voice in Standards for Evaluating

The typical evaluation is teacher-constructed. Teachers devise questions to answer, multiple-choice tests to complete, essays to compose, science lab tests to perform, and math problems to solve. Yet teachers often wonder whether everyone did their best. Weak test scores are often due to undermotivation. Many students do not care about their test scores or about whether or not they show what they learned from reading. Some teachers move motivation upward by affording students some participation, a voice in how their achievement is judged.

Teachers can give students a voice in standards for evaluating in science, among other subjects. In a neighboring high school, science teacher Allison had students create a rubric for a project on atoms. During this project, the students had to complete research on the atom, design an advertisement poster to "sell" the atom, and create a three-dimensional model of the atom. They then had to bring their posters and models to class for peer evaluations based upon the rubric. The class, with direction from the teacher, decided upon the components of the rubric.

During the activity, the students "created" the rubric by first brainstorming a list of evaluation criteria based upon the project guidelines. Next, Allison built the peer evaluation rubric based upon the class selections. She presented this rubric to the class and encouraged them to offer final revisions. Students then used these rubrics to complete the peer evaluations of the posters and models. Although this process was very time-intensive, Allison found that the students were more motivated to complete the project and participate in the peer evaluation. Allison's students had a clear sense of what was expected of them and what the evaluation criteria were for the project. They even began to build their own social support, asking each other questions about the project instead of coming to her first. The students became self-directed learners as they created their own rubric, completed the project, and graded one portion of the project.

Based upon her success with this project, Allison is trying this activity in other aspects of the class. For example, after reading a chapter in a book, the students will brainstorm a list of criteria or concepts that should be included on the chapter test. This could have enormous benefits for students' commitment to the importance and value of their evaluation.

Inquiry Projects

From talking to other teachers, we are familiar with many ways to put these practices together. We use the term "inquiry projects" to capture a variety of classwork that lifts students' self-direction. Here are two examples.

Middle school teacher Robert provides self-direction in social studies through his students' projects. Students are in control of the texts they use, the sequence in which they use them, and how they respond to what they have learned from the texts. This shows *ownership of text*. Of course, the text choices must relate to what they are learning in the curriculum. Before students begin a research project, Robert asks them to choose a specific topic from a list related to the course objectives. When his class did a project on ancient Egypt, students chose from a list of topics including religion, engineering, pharaohs, pyramids, warfare, art, and everyday life. One student who liked sports chose to do a project about how sports fit into the everyday lives of the ancient Egyptians. This shows *input into curriculum*.

Having defined their topics, the students went to the media center, where the specialist showed them how to effectively use the resources including books, Web sites, or any others available. This illustrates *providing options for how to learn*. Robert monitored the media center, gathering information about the students' progress and conversing with the students about their topics. Robert generally found that his students were either very amazed by the topic (like pyramids) or they found a connection to our times (such as art or warfare). Freedom in choice of topic and information sources was a very positive experience. Students became fully engaged in the texts they were using because they found them interesting.

After information was gathered, Robert gave his students a choice of presentation including a research paper, a play involving characters in Egypt, a physical representation of their research (such as a pyramid or a sphinx), or a videotape showing what they had learned. This exemplifies *self-selection of knowledge displays*. With a sense of autonomy (being in charge of oneself) comes the feeling of responsibility. Because students made a choice about what they read or how they conveyed their information, they had more of a stake in their product.

Scaffolding Control and Choice for Diverse Students

Diversity of students in the ability to manage self-direction is exceptionally wide. Above-grade level readers or advanced readers can self-direct a three-week project with an admirable outcome. They can successfully do the following: (1) set goals, (2) make outlines, (3) seek multimedia materials, (4) write profusely, (5) locate supplements, (6) critique with peers, and (7) follow a timeline. On-grade students cannot handle as much self-direction. The teacher may need to identify each step (1–7) for them. Nevertheless, they can make good choices and take control of reading and learning within each stage. Below-grade level readers are often even less self-directing. Teachers often assume this means they are incapable of any meaningful choices, which is not the case.

Lower achievers can make all the same decisions, but they frequently need very short menus and discussion about each alternative. Instead of simply being prompted to "make an outline of your project report," which might be sufficient for the above-grade students, lower achievers may require more support. For example, a teacher may offer the option of making an outline containing either three or four main points. This is a smaller, but nontrivial, choice. Thus, a teacher scaffolds the process of choosing and self-direction like she scaffolds the teaching of content.

Teachers who use choice to support engaged reading give students choices that tie into different aspects of balanced literacy instruction (e.g., vocabulary, fluency, strategy instruction, writing). Choices tied to vocabulary instruction include having English language learners (ELLs) choose what words to include in their "Academic Vocabulary Glossary." Experienced teachers may scaffold ELLs' choices with a "Word Bank" from which students can select words. When focusing on fluency instruction, students can choose their preferred practice format for expressive reading from the following:

- Tape recording and listening to their reading
- Reading to a partner and receiving feedback
- Echo reading

Strategy instruction can include simple choices such as what paragraph to summarize and what questions to ask, or more complex choices such as what strategy to use to show understanding of the main ideas of an expository book. Writing choices can include which character to react to in the last novel read, salient dimensions of child labor in a condemnation speech, or simply selecting which transition words to use from paragraph to paragraph in an essay. During independent reading time, students could also choose what book to read from a selected menu. With some planning, all components of a balanced literacy curriculum can be imbued with student choices (Taboada, Guthrie, & McRae, in press).

Choice is an empowering tool for ELL students and results in their increased engagement in text. When students choose what to read about within a given topic, what information to record during their observations, what questions to ask, and what to research for the culminating project, they know their choices are relevant to what they are learning. When students read to find answers to their questions, reading becomes a personal, focused experience. Students can become "experts" on a topic or a book. Specifically, struggling readers and English language learners gain the unique opportunity to have their peers consult them for their expertise on a topic. In this way, choice presents students with opportunities to grasp new academic challenges and tests the boundaries of their academic competencies (Stipek, 2002; Taboada, Guthrie, & McRae, in press).

Order in the Classroom!

Creating and maintaining order is a high priority in every classroom. Accomplishing this with energetic, social adolescents can be challenging. The challenge is severe if the students are marginally disengaged. In meeting this challenge, teachers necessarily set up a system of rewards and punishments. A fight deserves punishment. Not attending class has a cost. Not attending during a quiz has a higher penalty. On the other side, actions such as completing homework, writing clearly, being cooperative, meeting deadlines, and participating enthusiastically deserve rewards. A teacher's goal of motivating through self-direction has to enter onto this stage. Obviously, a teacher cannot share control 100% of the time. Totally open classrooms are not productive ones in most cases. In this context, sharing control is incremental. If a teacher holds 20 levers of power, she can invite students to operate one lever on one occasion. The teaching practices portrayed here represent some of these levers of power and control. Teachers can design how to introduce the sharing into the classroom process.

Certainly, punishments reduce misbehavior, and rewards will incite some students to read. These effects, however, are short term. When students read only for a reward, the reading stops once the student attains the reward. When a student defers his rowdy behavior in fear of punishment, he will get rowdy when the punishment is not present, perhaps because the teacher is not in the classroom or is not looking at him (Kohn, Bates, & Polyson, 1999). To accomplish the important aim of fostering student growth, teachers cannot afford to reduce reading to a mere tool for gaining goodies dispensed by a power figure. Teachers want to cultivate internal motivation that generates self-extending text interaction.

Roles for Administrators

Teachers are not the only educators responsible for students' reading. Administrators also play a vital role. If teachers are to empower students to take command of their reading, administrators need to share control with teachers. Although the idea of allowing teachers more "wiggle room" in their classrooms might seem frightening to most high school policy creators and principals, "when applied to what teachers need to help individual students—more time, more materials, and more opportunities to develop their expertise—it does not sound risky at all. It sounds like common sense" (G. Ivey, 2000, p. 44).

4

Reading Is Social

Bringing Peer Interaction to the Text

Dee Antonio and John T. Guthrie
University of Maryland

Adolescence is a time of social discovery. Many students are seeking their place in a social world. As they enter middle school, they face waves of individuals with a variety of sizes, shapes, and personalities. The human spectrum may be exciting, but it also may be threatening to more timid souls. As middle school progresses, students find new friends, activities, and contexts in their quest for connection. An increasingly electronic world magnifies their social network. After school, adolescents spin an intricate web with their friends through text messaging, Web chats, voice mail, cell phones, and live group chatter. They aspire to determine who they are and who they will become. By trying on possible selves in the social milieu, students slowly form the core of their interpersonal relationships.

The need for being connected that springs to life in middle school and expands through higher education can accelerate or impede students' academic literacy. Because social needs dominate over books and learning through print, students can easily form an identity as a light reader or nonreader. Motivation for reading declines, as social motivation rises (Otis,

Grouzet, & Pelletier, 2005). On the other side, when students find book-based interests such as history, literature, or drama, and share these with peers, their reading may be promoted.

When we refer to reading in this chapter, we are indicating the inter-action with longer, substantive text that is carrying subject matter knowledge or serious literature. The medium may be print or electronic, but in either case, we are referring to academic literacy. Although text messaging between friends is enjoyable and social, it does not confer deep knowledge of subject matter on the reader. Therefore, we are talking about the power of students' social and interpersonal needs to influence school reading and academic literacy.

We portray six instructional practices that invite expression of students' social tendencies and bring students into school reading: (1) *open discussions*, in which students converse directly with each other to uncover the meanings of text, (2) *student-led discussion groups* that allow individuals to interact with each other relatively freely, (3) *collaborative reasoning* that enables students to benefit from each other's thinking and perspectives, (4) *arranging partnerships* that can help to build a social scaffold for reading, (5) *socially constructing the management* that enhances students' sense of belonging to the school culture, and (6) *scaffolding social motivations over time* to enable adolescents to internalize the social goals and patterns of education.

Open Discussions

In every classroom, teachers hold discussions with students about subject matter and often about the readings or texts for the class. The question is whether the discussions involving teachers and the whole class are "open" or "closed" in verbal interchanges. The overwhelmingly dominant form of teacher-student interaction consists of the teacher posing a question, a student responding with an attempt to answer the question, and the teacher providing an evaluation about the appropriateness or accuracy of the answer. This has been termed the IRE pattern of interaction, in which the teacher initiates (I), the student replies (R), and the teacher evaluates (E). In contrast, open discussion usually begins with an open-ended question about which students can legitimately disagree. During open discussion, all participants, including teachers and students, are partners in developing an understanding of text. To sustain this discussion, teachers ask a reasonable proportion of questions that are not quickly or obviously answered. Teacher questions are authentic in the sense that they do not seek a prespecified answer; a right answer may not exist. Appropriate responses may vary depending upon the students' perspectives or opinions. In open discussion, many questions include uptake of previous comments. That is, one individual's question does not come out of nowhere, but is built on previous information and the interests of other participants in the discussion.

An example of a traditional discussion with an IRE pattern about Homer's *The Iliad* is presented next.

Teacher: According to the poet, what is the subject of *The Iliad*?
Mary: Achilles' anger.
Teacher: Where does the action of the first part of Book 1 take place when we enter the story?
Joshua: On the Achaean ship?
Teacher: Well, they are not on their ships. Let's see if we can give you a diagram.
Doreen: Was it on the shore?
Teacher: Yes, it's on the shore.

The teacher was leading the students to factual reconstruction of the plot with questions for which she had all the answers, based explicitly on the text.

Next, is an example of a more open discussion in a middle school classroom on Harper Lee's *To Kill a Mockingbird.* The class is discussing the ending when Bob Ewell attacks the children, but ends up dead.

Teacher: How does Bob Ewell get killed?
Daria: Boo Radley did it.
Teacher: How did you figure out that Boo killed him?
Daria: I guess I thought that the knife, I didn't really understand this part. I thought it was Boo at the beginning, but then I wasn't sure.
Ruthie: He said he doesn't want to reveal it to the sheriff because he would ruin Boo's life.
Wesley: Right.
Brandi: Even if he totally did it.
Jose: He'd get all this attention and he couldn't obviously avoid it.
Ruthie: No, he wouldn't be able to continue to live his life as before if they all found out that he did it.
Teacher: Why not?
Brandi: Well, he's going to have to go to trial and all this stuff and everyone will know that he has.
Daria: I think it's worth it.
Teacher: So you think that Hectate was wrong in covering up?
Jose: Yes, well Hectate said that anyway, it's going to be self-defense anyway; however, it comes up on the trial because you can really

argue it that way. So you have to go through the whole trial and then it will be up to the jury and stuff and get some answer that you already know about.

The teacher's role in this open discussion was one of directing the conversational traffic, focusing issues, and guiding students through the text to answer their own questions (Applebee, Langer, Nystrand, & Gamoran, 2003).

Open discussions can be held in many subject matters, including social studies. For example, one of our colleagues, Suzanne, taught a high school class titled "Principles of Law," in which students were introduced to the juvenile justice system. The students first read a chapter in their text about juvenile justice with the purpose of determining whether it is legitimate to try a juvenile as an adult. After reading, students played roles as a juvenile involved in criminal activity, court members, and judges. To build the role-playing interchange, Suzanne held an open discussion regarding the responsibilities of each member in the problem-based scenario. She required that the discussion be realistic and faithful to the text, but did not guide the questions or definitions of roles. In this scenario, students read deeply to form multiple perspectives about the juvenile justice system.

It is sensible to question how open discussions serve to motivate students' reading. In a discussion that is "open" by the previously stated standards, students feel important. Their ideas are recognized by other students and used as a basis for further interaction; they are not merely told whether their information is right or wrong. In an open discussion, students feel a higher sense of acceptance. Twists and turns of the interaction may follow their input. Talk does not simply involve someone's judgments about correctness of every point that is made. Being accepted confers a sense of "relatedness" to students, which is critical to their adolescent development (Ryan & Deci, 2000b).

Student-Led Discussions

Our colleague Melissa, a middle school English teacher, uses literature discussion groups in her classroom. For example, she teaches the novel *Call Me Ruth* by Marilyn Sachs in conjunction with a unit about immigration to America in the late nineteenth century. Before beginning reading, she helps the students to preview the book, looking at the front and back covers. Students then predict what they feel the book will be about, based on these clues. Along with prediction, students analyze the setting of this text. After reading the first chapter, Melissa guides the students to identify and connect the setting to information about late nineteenth-century America. For each chapter, the students keep a journal of main events and the characters' motivations. In class discussions, students exchange what is happening and how the characters relate to each other. Melissa provides the goal of comparing and contrasting the events and characters to contemporary times, and individual groups form their own interpretations of the book in these terms. One homework assignment is to go to an immigration Web site, locate the experience of one family, and compare that experience to the events in the novel. In the literature discussion group, there is the organizational structure of a leader who starts and stops the events, and a summarizer who notes important points made by each person in the discussion. Melissa monitors the interactions to assure full participation by all members, and whole class discussions are held to avoid any groups falling seriously off track. These interactions are exciting for students and make them want to be engaged in the classroom.

In a survey of studies on more than a dozen types of small group discussion interactions, Wilkinson (2006) reported that student-led discussions had higher impact on student engagement than teacher-led discussions did. In student-led discussions, there was higher participation, enthusiasm, reading prior to discussion, and depth of thought than there was in teacher-led discussions. An explanation for this advantage of student-led discussions is that students are motivated by being in control of their activities. Although the text may be preidentified by the teacher, and overarching issues may be established by the curriculum, the student-led discussion enables individuals to be at least partially in charge of their interchange, subquestions, and conclusions. It is well-established that when students possess a relatively high measure of perceived control in their classroom interactions, they are more highly engaged in reading and talking than when students are completely directed by the teacher or the program (Furrer & Skinner, 2003).

Adolescents' social motivations are starkly evident in their patterns of Internet use. After school, they hurry home, often departing from a peer, to join a chat room. In this briskly interactive social space, they sustain multiple simultaneous conversations. They may also talk on the phone at the same time. Such networking often lasts hours, and they only reluctantly give it up. In school reading endeavors, this electronic communication pattern is also effective. We have seen a book club that meets on the Internet, a science group of insect buffs who load photos into a Web site, and a Spanish course that writes and reads in a chat room. Teachers who tap into the social appeal of electronic communication can foster student-led discussion that is text based and educationally productive.

Collaborative Reasoning

When we set up social interaction around text in the classroom, we seek to go beyond a mere exchange of opinion. Talk for its own sake may or may not be text-based, and may or may not benefit the students' reading comprehension. To improve students' reading comprehension through dialogue, it is important to move groups, whole classes, or teams toward collaborative reasoning. Based on information from the text, we want students developing an argument, rather than merely tossing out an opinion. An argument is composed of three main ingredients: (1) a claim, (2) a reason for the claim, and (3) evidence for the reason. In reading a novel, history text, or science book, students can build arguments collaboratively by identifying claims, reasons, and evidence, which is usually—but not necessarily—in the text (Chinn, Anderson, & Waggoner, 2001).

In an eighth-grade social studies classroom in Pennsylvania, forty students developed arguments about the theme "Violence in Our Culture." Specific groups focused on topics of terrorism and violence in schools, the media, and the individual. Each group attempted to read a variety of texts to boost their knowledge on the topic, including books such as Lois Lowry's *The Giver* and excerpts from psychologists like Sigmund Freud. They identified types of violence (claims), causes of the violence (reasons), and examples from historical, scientific, or literary sources (evidence). The teacher acted like a facilitator, helping students work through the text to create their arguments together. The teacher claimed that this process led the students to become extremely self-directed in all aspects of the curriculum, with a positive view of learning from text (Brown, 2002).

One way to help students collaboratively reason from text is to help them make their arguments highly explicit. To do this, teachers draw students' attention to the three features of claims, reasons, and evidence. Some student teams, who are attempting to build a good argument, may set reasoning subgoals consisting of claims and counterclaims. They may form subgoals of locating evidence *for* a claim and evidence that *contradicts* the same claim. Of course, a teacher or students could model the strategy of forming an argument by reading a brief passage and, identifying a claim, reasons, and evidence in the passage to support it. In all cases, as the quality of discussion rises, the comprehension of text increases accordingly (Chinn et al., 2001).

Collaborative reasoning is motivating because of its connection to self-determination theory (Ryan & Deci, 2000a). Beyond being competent, students have fundamental needs to believe in their competence. As students hone the processes of forming good arguments, and perhaps as they win a few text-based arguments, they gain a sense of competence in comprehending text deeply. Although a claim or the identification of an important reason can be based solely on personal preferences, students' development of viewpoints can also follow traditional lines of syllogistic reasoning. This is the essence of good thinking based on text. When students perform collaborative reasoning, they are thinking in a group based on knowledge gained from reading. On this journey, students simultaneously extend their knowledge and their social interaction processes.

Why Social Interaction? Research and Theory

Our claim in this chapter is that social interaction surrounding reading is motivating to students. Although this is a broad claim, a substantial amount of evidence supports this viewpoint. In one study, Furrer and Skinner (2003) looked at all aspects of this assertion. They asked students specifically whether they felt accepted, special, noticed, and important, with respect to their teacher, classmates, and friends. Students who scored highly on this measure felt a sense of belonging or "relatedness" to their social partners.

Students with a sense of relatedness were deeply engaged in their classrooms. Teachers reported them as enthusiastic and actively participating. In contrast, some students were feeling that they did not belong and were experiencing a sense of not being related to the classroom. Teachers rated them as appearing frustrated and disconnected from classroom activities.

Students also reported their own engagement. Those with a high sense of relatedness were likely to say, "I participate when we discuss new material." On the other side, students who felt alienated were likely to say, "In class, I just act like I'm working," or "I feel mad in this class." Feeling related to others was connected to active engagement in reading and classroom activities. Students' academic performance was also linked. If students felt highly related to the teacher and their peers, their academic performance, which consisted of grades in reading and other subjects, was higher than the performance of students who felt unrelated and isolated (Furrer & Skinner, 2003).

One may question why students' social lives should connect to their reading in the classroom. After all, reading is basically a solitary activity and depends on individual initiative and attention. One explanation for the role of interpersonal interaction in reading is that social interaction is a basic need. When the need for relatedness is filled by feeling connected to others, students prosper (Guthrie, Schafer, Wang, & Afflerbach, 1995). Conversely, if the social disposition is not met because students are isolated, alienated, or unnoticed, then students are likely to feel frustrated. Their frustration may accumulate and develop into anger or animosity toward the teacher or the classroom.

In one investigation, Assor, Kaplan, and Kanat-Maymon (2005) observed that the frustration of social needs led to anger and anxiety in the classroom. Some students reported that the teacher often interrupted them, prevented them from doing what they were interested in, and rejected their opinions about topics. These students felt alienated and isolated from the social flow of the classroom. They felt hostility toward the teacher. It is fascinating that the students did not merely fall into a passive state of apathy. Rather, they took active means to defend their sense of who they were and became aggressive toward the teacher and other students. Likewise, Furrer and Skinner (2003) found that students who were feeling neglected and not belonging reported not apathy, but "feeling mad" at the teacher, as well as being emotionally disaffected.

This need for relatedness is innate or inborn, according to theorists Ryan and Deci (2000b). They have argued that we are "social animals," born with the disposition to be a group member, join with others, and develop interpersonal bonds. According to this viewpoint, when these needs are fulfilled, we prosper, and if suffocated, we suffer a loss of well-being.

Social motivations may also be a source of energy and direction. According to this theory, it is not that we have a need and suffer if it is not met; rather, we enjoy the benefits of social interaction if they are afforded to us. Consistent with this view, researcher Wentzel (1991) observed that students who desired to get along well with others in the classroom and who contributed positively to classroom routines achieved high reading grades and test scores. She termed these students *prosocial* because they wanted to promote goodwill, good feelings, positive dialogue, and smoothly flowing routines in the classroom. She distinguished the prosocial goals from the students' desires to belong to the group and feel the security of group membership. Both of these qualities—prosocial goals and belonging—separately contribute to students' motivation for academic achievement in a classroom.

Social motivation promotes success in reading by providing a human safety net. Students who form close friends have a sense of mutual trust with others. Their interpersonal closeness is a source of strength in the face of academic challenges such as understanding long, complex texts and performing well in textbook-based learning activities. Students with friends and interpersonal connections show resilience in times of challenge or even failure. They can gain concrete information and personal reassurance about conquering academic challenges such as difficult text and formidable reading lists. Thus, interpersonal bonds serve students at many levels in the schooling process (Davis, 2003).

Arranging Partnerships

There are myriad opportunities for students to read together in pairs within a classroom. One frequent reason for such pairing is that students often face texts that require a second thought and a second pair of eyes. Teachers often assign pairs based on the seating plan or ability matching by general achievement in the class. Pairs read a critical portion of text—for example, one to five pages—to identify key elements such as characters, symbols, embedded meanings, or higher-order interpretations. In pairs, students complete tasks to share with the whole class or team. Simultaneously, students may write their reactions to the text in the form of a journal. This simple partnering gives students an opportunity to be actively social and to avoid exposure to possible embarrassment in front of the whole class.

Formal peer tutoring in a classroom is also possible in reading. Peer tutoring may not seem to be the most practical means to implementing reading strategies. However, with some time invested, teachers can make use of a system to deliver their content and make their students more competent, interested readers. PALS (peer-assisted learning strategies) is a peer tutoring strategy which pairs higher-performing students with lower-performing students to work on a set of structured reading activities. During each PALS session, the tutor-tutee pairs work through three structured activities: (1) partner reading with retell, (2) paragraph shrinking, and (3) prediction relay. During the first activity, each student reads aloud from connected text for five minutes. The teacher provides text at an appropriate level for the tutee in each pair. The higher-performing student reads first, followed by the lower-performing student reading the same text. Whenever the reader makes an error, the tutor says, "Stop, you missed a word. Can you figure it out?" If the reader does not figure out the word quickly, the tutor says, "That word is X." The reader then says the word and continues reading. After both students have read, the lower-performing student retells the sequence of events. Students earn one point for each sentence read correctly, and ten points for the retell (McMaster, D. Fuchs, & L. S. Fuchs, 2006).

The second activity in PALS, paragraph shrinking, is designed to develop comprehension through summarization and main idea identification. Students use a questioning strategy to direct their attention to important ideas. During paragraph shrinking, the students continue reading orally, but stop at the end of each paragraph to identify its main idea. The tutor asks the reader to identify the main idea. The reader must "shrink" this information into 10 words or fewer. If the tutor determines the answer is incorrect, he simply says, "That's not right. Skim the paragraph and try again." After five minutes, the pair switches roles (McMaster et al., 2006).

The final activity, prediction relay, requires students to make predictions and then identify whether they are confirmed or not. Prediction relay consists of four steps: (1) making a prediction about what will happen on the next half page, (2) reading the half page aloud, (3) confirming or not confirming the prediction, and (4) summarizing the main idea. If the tutor disagrees with the prediction, he says, "I don't agree. Think of a better prediction." The pair switches roles after five minutes.

Researchers L. S. Fuchs, D. Fuchs, and Kazdan (1999) analyzed the effects of PALS on students' reading performance. They focused on high school students reading at the second- through sixth-grade levels. They followed 18 special education and remedial reading high school teachers for 16 weeks. Nine teachers provided instruction in PALS and nine teachers offered individual, small group teaching. Throughout the 16-week period, teachers implemented their respective instruction with all students in their classes. PALS teachers supplemented their instruction five times every two weeks for 16 weeks. After the 16-week period, students in the PALS treatment group improved their reading comprehension scores significantly more than the students in the comparison group did. In addition, students in PALS reported working harder and had more positive beliefs about their reading than students in the comparison group had. This model appears to support the social interaction, as well as the reading competencies, of lower-achieving high school students (L. S. Fuchs et al., 1999).

Although we have not used this exact model, variants of it have proved useful in our classes. For instance, when introducing a new unit, instead of lecturing and providing notes for background information, we prefer to find six or seven short, readable passages that cover the important points. Then, we form trios rather than pairs. Each group must read together. Groups either rotate to different stations to read each passage and complete a task, or if time is short, each group reports back to the class on their topic. We find that such small groups remove students' fears about reading in front of others. They really do end up helping each other, rather than making fun of others, which can be all too common during class reading time.

Research has emphasized the benefits of having English language learners (ELLs) collaborate using reading strategies to improve reading comprehension in the form of modified reciprocal teaching methods (Klingner & Vaughn, 1996). If collaboration is to support engaged reading for ELLs, these children need opportunities to be exposed to the English language by their English-speaking peers, as well as to engage in oral and written communication themselves. To benefit completely from social interactions, ELLs need to be actively participating in oral conversations, as well as reading and writing activities, where both academic vocabulary and conceptual knowledge are at the heart.

Partnering activities give students an opportunity to be actively social around literacy endeavors. Struggling readers and ELLs benefit from partnerships that can provide a secure context where they can practice skills and strengthen knowledge before they are ready to face the whole class. Overall, social interactions should be arranged so students have a voice in the ways of working with texts, and have opportunities to exchange knowledge and opinions with others. When teachers create a socially cohesive climate where most students become active participants, students become more committed, excited, and enthusiastic about literacy (Taboada, Guthrie, & McRae, in press).

These partnership arrangements provide a social scaffold for developing reading competence. Students can work in two- or three-person groups—either with similar levels of ability or with distinct ability levels—with less fear and anxiety than they may feel in the whole class situation. Although pairs must be monitored for productivity, and points may be awarded to initialize pair productivity, this interaction can meet students' need for relatedness, and thus, improve reading interest.

Socially Constructing Class Management

A growing body of evidence about teacher-student relationships reveals that students are sensitive to opportunities for contributing to the "game plan" in class. When students are consulted in decision making about texts, the ways in working with them, and student interactions about text, they feel stronger commitment to literacy work. There are many ways in which the roles of texts in learning can be negotiated with students. This does not imply that students have the entitlement to banish books from a course. It signifies that there are legitimate, alternative uses of books. There are ways to involve students in weaving the literacy demands through the social patterns in the classroom. By involving students in decision making, teachers elicit higher student investment to the content of the course (Davis, 2003).

Decisions and management judgments that can be negotiated with students include the following and many more:

- Seating arrangements in a classroom
- Disciplinary actions against students who are absent, late, or disruptive
- The sequence of instructional activities, which may include a menu such as (a) read, write, pair discussion, (b) read, pair discussion, write, and (c) pair discussion, read, write

- A menu of subtopics for student discussion and selection. If it is reasonable to have 12 subtopics for a unit, more time might be devoted to some (as specializations) than others, and students can contribute to decisions about time and give their rationales for importance of their selections
- Time spent on different class activities; for instance, a 45-minute period might be divided into three 15-minute portions, or two portions of 10 minutes each and one portion of 25 minutes for such activities as lecture, small group discussion, and discussion about writing
- Alternative texts may be used for a given topic; suppose texts A, B, and C were used for a topic within a unit. Students could discuss whether all individuals read all texts or whether there is an alternative. One alternative may be that one-third reads text A, one-third reads text B, and one-third reads text C. Students reading a different text make a group report to the class, which is responsible for learning all of the parts. The class could discuss the advantages and disadvantages of the two approaches, consisting of all students reading all texts, or subgroups reading subsets
- Teacher-student co-construction of quizzes (e.g., five short essays and 15 multiple-choice items) with the teacher composing half of the items and the class members writing the other half. The class can discuss how to divide the task and compose the final quiz

Within each classroom, the requirements, rights, and obligations of each student must be determined. A teacher can create a more socially cohesive climate by involving students in some decisions. The balance is delicate. Affording too many decisions to students may be irresponsible, and may increase student anxiety. On the other side, affording too few opportunities for personal construction of the social fabric of the classroom generates a cold, hostile environment to individuals who want to participate in a social environment they are co-constructing.

In a collaborative classroom, the teacher acts as a mediator for student engagement with reading and literacy. Successful mediating involves creating a classroom environment that promotes active participation for the widest possible majority. For example, rearranging students' desks so they face each other encourages verbal interchange and sharing of ideas. Moving the teacher's desk to a less prominent area of the classroom enables students to feel more comfortable to work freely with each other.

In a "Historical Trends and Technology" class, the teacher relocated her desk from the front of the classroom to a side area. She also rearranged the students' desks in rows facing each other, with an open space in the middle of both sides. She found this to be more conducive to collaborative activities because students can see each other as they exchange various concepts. Students also are more relaxed in this class since the teacher is less prominent. This classroom arrangement allows students to easily and freely work together on a regular basis.

Our colleague Amy teaches biology in a neighboring high school. Amy's class created a crime scene investigation (CSI) with each student researching and choosing a specific role (detective, EMT, coroner, police officer, sketch artist, etc.) to play in the investigation. In her classes, Amy consistently allows students to self-direct their methods of learning and displaying their knowledge, guiding them in this process. In this unit, she encouraged students to make videos, interview, and write about the specific role each of them would play in the investigation. The students created many assignments along the way to show their progress and to clarify how their roles fit into the investigation. More important, the assessments showed that the students could make connections between the oral investigation and the genetics unit as a whole, which was devoted to DNA and how speciation depends on mutations. Students worked with peers who were researching the same role. At the end of their investigation, the class presented the crime scene to an audience of middle school students.

The activity was highly motivating for biology students. Social negotiation took place on all levels. Within their teams, students debated what type of information they needed to fulfill their roles, how to locate the information, and how to display the presentation. They collaborated to solve the CSI case using their best reasoning capabilities. The teacher served as an arbitrator for how to solve disputes and an ombudsman for a few students who needed support. This project met students' needs for belonging, relatedness, and prosocial goals, combined with academic goals for learning from text in this biology unit.

Scaffolding Social Motivation Over Time

Following is an in-depth example of a successful model for social interaction in science inquiry. Amy, our colleague who carried out the successful CSI unit in her biology class in the previous example, used the genetic disorder cystic fibrosis (CF), as a science problem for inquiry. She asked the students to place themselves in the role of a professional in the field of genetics. From different perspectives, the students actively explored the open-ended problem of cystic fibrosis to generate solutions to its various effects on patients and communities. Amy first helped students activate prior knowledge about CF by using a chart to identify what was known and what was needed to be known in various fields. Students listed the facts they knew, the ones they wanted to learn, and their action plan for collecting information. They were asked to assume a role such as a genetic counselor or a pregnant woman carrying the cystic fibrosis gene. By selecting such a personally poignant role, they identified with the problems generated by CF. The teacher showed a short video of a young child with cystic fibrosis, which prompted the class to read widely and deeply about the medical condition.

Amy expected the students to summarize text about cystic fibrosis and write their reactions to the text from the viewpoint of the role they were playing. They attempted to solve the open-ended problem that they constructed from their role in collaboration with other students. Last, students were expected to create either a PowerPoint presentation or perform a skit that showed what they learned about this genetic disorder. Students were expected to form partnerships with other students in their same roles, to share text information, and to critique each other's reading and writing as the project progressed (Goodnough & Cashion, 2003).

The previous example displays a high level of social negotiation in reading and writing. Although the students navigated these decisions and resolved conflicts after several opportunities to learn in such a complex unit, teacher guidance was needed. The project could not have been accomplished without scaffolding across time provided by the teacher. Table 4.1 follows 14 elements in this class project, beginning with the unit theme, continuing to subtopics and activity frameworks for studying the theme, and concluding with giving a class presentation to an audience. On the right side of the chart are scaffolds A, B, C, and X, provided by the teacher. Scaffolds A, B, and C show the transition from high teacher guidance to lower teacher guidance. Scaffold X represents the example at the beginning of this section for cystic fibrosis. In scaffold X, it is evident that the teacher chose the unit theme, but students selected subtopics within the theme, incorporating interaction between themselves, the teacher, and others. The teacher and students negotiated the roles of groups and the teacher provided one text; students found other texts for themselves. On the topics of representing the content, displaying knowledge, and critiquing each other, students were expected to discuss these aspects with others and to cooperatively direct their work. This level of social self-direction may have occurred in March of an academic year. However, to get to this point, the teacher provided scaffolds A, B, and C earlier in the year. In the first class project of this kind, the teacher provided scaffold A, in which she decided the theme, subtopics, opportunity framework, and roles of groups. The teacher and students each had 50% input into texts, Web sites, and the other elements. Even at the beginning of the school year, students were encouraged to make decisions about the knowledge displays, the production, and the audience for their work. Thus, as the chart shows, scaffolding for social motivation began with the teacher expecting students to socially negotiate about one-half of the project, while she made decisions for the other half. Toward the end of the year, student social negotiation was dominant for nearly all parts of the project.

Table 4.1 illustrates that teachers raise the bar for higher levels of student input into management of reading and learning as the year progresses.

Table 4.1   Scaffolding Motivation Over Time

Class Project Elements	Scaffold A (high)	Scaffold B (medium)	Scaffold C (low)	Scaffold X (example)
Unit theme	T	T	T	T
Subtopics	T	T/S	T/S	S
Activity framework	T	T/S	T/S	T
Roles of groups	T	T/S	T/S	T/S
Roles of individuals	S	S	S	S
Texts	T	T/S	S	T/S
Web sites/videos	T	T/S	S	T
Representing content to groups	S	T/S	S	S
Planning knowledge displays	S	S	S	S
Producing knowledge displays	S	S	S	S
Identifying and delivering to audience	S	S	S	S
Critique learning and reading	T/S	T/S	S	S
Critique writing	T/S	T/S	S	S
Critique presentation	T/S	T/S	S	S

Note: T = Teacher; S = Student

5

Self-Efficacy

Building Confident Readers

Shana Yudowitch, Lucas M. Henry, and John T. Guthrie
University of Maryland

Self-confidence may seem to be a luxury in reading. If students can read our course materials well, why should we be concerned with their confidence? For the able students who perform well, self-confidence is not a worry. Excellent students usually have high self-confidence and believe in themselves. Their confidence is built from their success.

On the other side, for many students, the course readings are intimidating. Perhaps it is the vocabulary, the sheer size of a textbook, or the complexity of the content. But often, students doubt their ability to read the materials for a course. Some doubters are struggling readers who have been low achievers for years. Other students may be on-grade level on a standardized test, but the textbook, nevertheless, seriously overwhelms them.

A downward spiral can quickly set in. Suppose a student faces a large, colorful, complex, challenging history textbook. After reading two to three pages, the student is really lost. He sees a few facts and a few pictures, but he knows he did not gain the gist. He realizes he could not report the main ideas of those pages. Perhaps it is worse. Suppose he cannot read the pages aloud, and fails to identify 5 to 10 words or names on each page. Suddenly, he loses confidence. He feels that "I can't do it." He says, "This book is impossible for me." His effort wanes, and he may not complete the first assignment. He may actually be capable of reading and doing the assignment, but he feels inept. He doubts his capacity, which is the definition of low self-efficacy. Thus, he disengages from this text at this time.

This student may attend class, and may even answer a few questions, based on his listening skills, but the downward spiral has set in. Lacking self-efficacy, he will avoid the text, which is the main source of knowledge, quiz scores, class discussions, and a passing grade. As he shuns the text, he may rescue his reputation with classmates by saying that he does not study, and therefore, expects to fail quizzes. By avoiding the text, he prevents his own learning and precludes himself from improving in reading. As an increasingly marginal reader, his disengagement from the text grows. His school attendance may even be threatened.

The downward spiral of low self-efficacy, avoidance, lack of reading development, and stunted knowledge growth is dangerous. It imperils the student and dispirits the teacher. To reverse this spiral is possible, but not simple. If converting this spiral to an upward direction was effortless, students would not retreat from textbooks, homework, course involvement, and school commitment as often as they do.

We present five instructional practices that address the self-efficacy of students in our classrooms. These practices can work in concert or can be adopted separately. Our first job in improving self-efficacy is to *recognize the gap* between our students and their texts. Next, we match the text to the reading levels of our students. We then get the students reading comfortably with the material we located, which we call *establishing initial confidence*. Following, we teach *setting realistic goals* they can reach with this text, and help them recognize their success. To help students meet their goals, we spend time *assuring the enabling skills* for comprehending the text. In the middle of this chapter, we present the theory and research on instructional support for building self-efficacy in reading.

Recognizing the Gap

Once students develop the ability to read the words on the page, it is critical that teachers not turn them off to reading by using texts beyond their capabilities. As students become proficient decoders, teachers must foster this newfound ability as a means of increasing reading comprehension. To help catalyze this process, schools must be prepared to offer struggling readers books that are at or near their *actual* reading level, as well as books that are of interest to them.

One of the first roadblocks that teachers face as they try to foster literacy in their students is outright resistance. Many students we teach have become so disenfranchised from school, teachers, and reading that they completely shut down the instant reading becomes the focus of the class. Overcoming this hurdle is not an easy task, but it is one that school districts can help facilitate. We try to persuade administrators that handing students textbooks that are five to eight levels beyond their reading ability will only reinforce their avoidance of reading. Instead, these students must be given developmentally appropriate materials—books and stories written at or just above a child's current reading level—"to build decoding, word analysis, fluency, and reading comprehension strategies sequentially" (Dole, Brown, & Trathen, 1996).

In our school's well-meaning but haphazard way of trying to bring literacy to the students, the administration seems to think that building on prior knowledge and generating inferences will somehow magically make the difference. Not only is this prior knowledge frequently lacking, it is often erroneous (which is actually worse!). As a history teacher, the textbook is the primary source for imparting information to our students. But if the textbook is not suitable to the students' level of reading, it is not going to be particularly helpful.

On several occasions, we have had the opportunity to choose a textbook for our high school students. The first time, it was a government book for students in the struggling readers' program. Since the book closest to most of their reading levels was at the seventh- to eighth-grade level, it took a lot of looking, but we finally came up with *Jedi Mind Trick* by Finley, which looked like it belonged in a high school setting. It covered most of the government curriculum topics, yet accommodated the reading level of most of the students (fourth to fifth grade).

Teachers in every content use texts as a resource in the learning process. Unfortunately, the majority of high school students are not proficient readers. This fact, compounded with poor quality texts and time constrictions, make using texts a daunting task. From our experiences, we have recognized two main issues students have when learning from text. First, the available texts are poorly constructed and are difficult for high school students to read. Second, the texts are not written from the perspective of a high school student. Students have misunderstandings regarding content. If those misunderstandings are not addressed, the text fails to engage the students' prior knowledge; if a text only supplies information, and does not engage students in higher-order thinking, how can teachers get teenagers interested in reading texts and make the experience of reading advantageous to their purpose?

Expository texts assume students can use their prior knowledge to formulate meaning when reading. If students' prior knowledge is incorrect, their ability to understand many expository texts diminishes. In addition, many texts present concepts in fragmented pieces, rather than in a connected body of knowledge, and introduce concepts without discussing them in detail (Dole, 2000). These disadvantages not only limit students' learning of the quality and quantity of content, they do not support the development of new vocabulary for student learners nor address possible misconceptions. Therefore, it can be argued that all three factors—lack of knowledge, incompatible knowledge, and text structure—conspire to induce merely surface processing of science text that cannot support significant learning or the restructuring of preconceptions (Diakidoy, Kendeou, & Ioannides, 2003). In other words, students are not capable of creating meaning or of comprehending current science texts when there is lack of prior knowledge, possession of incorrect prior knowledge, and confusing text structure.

The motivational impact of this gap between the student and the text can be devastating. When students think the text is impossible to read, they lose confidence. They doubt their capacity to read that material, which is not irrational. Having been punished by attempting to read the text, they avoid it. They neglect homework, take short cuts, read minimally, and may abandon books for that course. At best, they attempt to take another pathway to learning, like listening closely in class, which is vastly insufficient for success.

Avoiding texts in a course has two ruinous effects. First, in a subject such as history, it is impossible to gain adequate knowledge without reading. Text-resistant students will languish in conceptual development in most subject matters. We have observed this statistically in a study. As Figure 5.1 shows, students began the school year with a pretest in knowledge about science. Within the total group, the intrinsically motivated students gained knowledge about science from September to December. They learned much from reading widely and deeply. Tragically, the reading-resistant students gained absolutely no science knowledge from September to December. Because other students were learning, they actually declined relative to their classmates. These reading-resistant students almost precluded themselves from future science learning by entering this long, dormant period of nonreading.

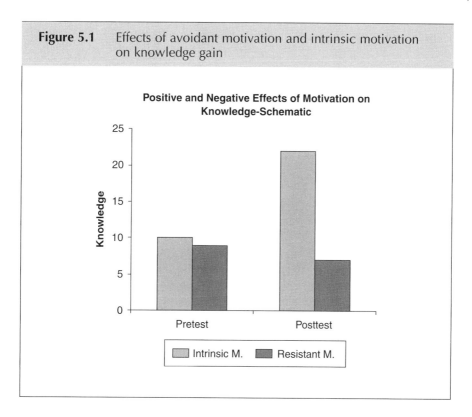

Figure 5.1 Effects of avoidant motivation and intrinsic motivation on knowledge gain

An even more injurious effect of resistance is lack of reading development. If a student goes three months with no improvement in reading, she actually declines. Relative to her peers who are increasing in reading comprehension, she slides backwards. We observed this statistically as well. In the same study of science reading, students who were intrinsically motivated gained in reading comprehension from September to December. Regrettably, the resistant students did not gain at all in reading grade equivalent. As a result, they declined in comparison to their peers. Figure 5.2 shows this negative impact of nonreading. Much of this resistance is due to diminished self-efficacy, as we previously suggested. Thus, the downward spiral of (1) inability to read class text, (2) lowered self-efficacy, (3) resistance, (4) nonreading, and (5) relative losses of knowledge and achievement are evident.

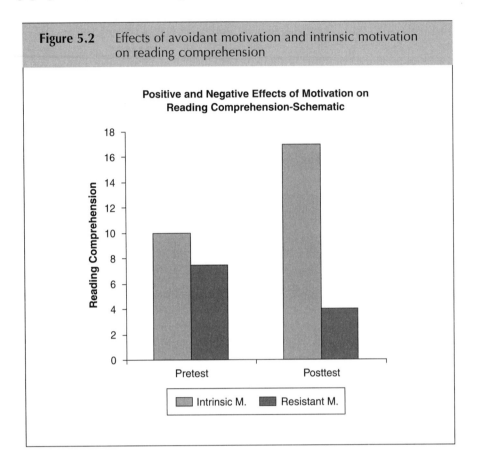

Figure 5.2   Effects of avoidant motivation and intrinsic motivation on reading comprehension

We provide an eye-opening view of the gap between students and texts in Resource A. This view shows texts on the National Assessment of Educational Progress (NAEP) that students could not handle. For Grades 8 and 12 separately, we located texts on the assessment that were beyond the reach of basic students (struggling readers), and proficient readers (on-grade readers, but not advanced ones). We placed these passages from the NAEP test next to excerpts from typical textbooks in English and science for Grades 8 and 12. It is quite obvious that Grade 8 students who failed the sample passage on the NAEP test would be extremely unlikely to be able to read the Grade 8 passages in typical English and science texts; it would be even more obvious for Grade-12 students. The classroom texts are far beyond the comprehension level of even the proficient (on-grade) students. The basic (below-grade) students have little chance of coping with them. The gap is evident, and it is nationwide.

Matching Text to Students

When we have a gap between students and texts, we take a big step. We match text to the students' reading levels. This is our tallest challenge in supporting students' self-efficacy for reading. But without this step, the students will miss the vast majority of our class offerings, and they may enter the downward spiral. Locating matched text may require switching textbooks. It may demand finding easy-to-read versions of literature. To make the match of student-to-text, we may offer alternative texts to some students. We may reach for Web sites or trade books to supplement the formidable class textbook.

In English, can we willingly hand our 10th-grade student a Dr. Seuss book just because it is on his reading level? Won't this exchange have a greater impact on the student's ego than on his reading skills? Again, those who instruct struggling readers in high school are put in an awkward situation.

There is a relatively simple answer to this problem. High-interest books that are readable are available to struggling middle and high school students. To encourage reluctant readers to read, schools must be willing to invest in nontraditional texts. Walter Dean Myers, for instance, writes novels that are usually on a fifth-grade reading level, but the content is designed to interest high school readers (see Resource B). Two of his novels, *Monster* and *Hoops,* not only look like books that an on-level high school student would read, but they follow teenage protagonists who investigate issues important to teenagers (Liang, 2002).

Some may argue that providing struggling readers with texts that are near their already-deficient reading levels will not accelerate their skills; it will only sustain the achievement gap. Recent studies have shown, however, that the use of texts that are near the reading level of struggling students does more to close this gap than presenting them with texts that are on their actual grade level does. O'Connor and colleagues (2002) documented the effects of teaching struggling readers with reading level texts (RLT) and class level texts (CLT). Students who were taught with texts that were at or near their reading level improved their reading fluency more than students taught with grade-level texts did. Among the weakest students, those with RLT showed greater gains than those with CLT (O'Connor et al., 2002).

Skeptics may argue that such practices may lead to gains in some areas, but ultimately, will not help a student's comprehension skills. This study also reported no significant differences between RLT students and CLT students regarding the quality of their reading comprehension. Although this study was limited in its scope, and focused on younger students, it is an avenue that deserves further attention, especially for the seemingly unreachable older students.

We find it difficult to step outside the bounds of the prescribed curriculum. But the bottom line is that we all want our students to be engaged in their reading. Several years ago, to our amazement, one of our students who hadn't read a word all year was suddenly engrossed in a book. How could we tell him to put his book down because we were working on something else? The educational system must remember one of the simplest tenets when trying to get through to an unwilling student: People are much more likely to be engaged and to enjoy what they are reading if they are capable of handling it easily. How can we ignore this?

We have difficulty presenting students with books in which themes revolve around gang life, drug use, and other bad habits merely because they are easy to read. However, high-interest, readable books do not have to contain such bad examples. Studies have shown that multicultural literature can be extremely engaging for students, regardless of their ethnicity or socioeconomic background. Multicultural literature that is readable can be located. These texts have the potential to motivate students by describing scenarios that may echo their own experiences. By presenting such texts in an open forum, teachers can foster personal discussions and increase the likelihood of debate, the understanding of others, and the ability to develop voice (Bean, Senior, Valerio, & White, 1999).

Using high-interest, readable books is critical for struggling readers with decoding difficulties and for ELLs who are limited in their English proficiency, but who have well-developed cognitive abilities. Using books with controlled vocabulary, low-reading level, and low-interest topics are detrimental to these students' reading self-efficacy, and ultimately, to their reading achievement. When teachers and schools spend the time, money, and effort on selecting texts that can be matched to students' reading levels and interests, students are more motivated to spend their own time, effort, and enthusiasm in learning from them.

Many ELLs come from cultures where they are not accustomed to ask questions about texts or other sources of knowledge (Haynes, 2007), so providing them with concrete steps helps them in the process. Second, teachers adjust text to the strategies students are learning. So if students are learning to search information texts, teachers ensure that books have a table of contents, an index, and a glossary that lend themselves to searching. A third way most teachers help students develop confidence in strategy use is by providing multiple opportunities for strategy practice, both across texts and genres.

The other important avenue to foster initial confidence in reading can be paved by helping students become fluent readers. Fluency is a bridge to comprehension, but it is also a fundamental element of students' self-efficacy in reading. Many struggling readers and ELLs are highly self-conscious of their oral reading and of whether or not their words sound "smooth" and fluent to others. When teachers pair these students with fluent readers and ensure that feedback is provided on prosody, intonation, and smooth reading, they are providing them with opportunities to become more confident readers. Fostering fluency and strategic reading are initial steps in helping students gain the self-efficacy they need to become engaged readers (Taboada, Guthrie, & McRae, in press).

In science, one way to address the gap of textbook and student reading level is to use supplementary materials. Science students are often unmotivated to read science textbooks because they are dense with terminology that does not seem to directly relate to their lives. Teachers can reduce this apathy toward reading by connecting scientific concepts to activities that are related to the students' lives (Guthrie & Davis, 2003).

One such example provided by Eichinger (2003) used tabloid science articles prior to the study of nuclear energy. Teachers can use these *exciting* articles to teach students how to analyze a passage for validity and credibility, which is an essential skill for all high school students in this age of conducting Internet research. In addition, students can practice reading strategies such as summarizing while reading the more *interesting* material.

The article "Bat Boy Saves Washington from Dirty Bomb Disaster" (Eichinger, 2003) is a good *hook* before beginning a text chapter on nuclear energy. Students are exposed to new vocabulary terms in the reading and can then analyze the claims of the article and how the author supports these claims. They complete this analysis in small groups with a teacher-created guide sheet including the following questions:

- How would you summarize the article in a few words?
- Which aspects of the article are believable and which are not?
- How do you know?
- What evidence does the author use to support his claims?
- How could you cross-check the veracity of these claims?
- What conclusions can you make about the accuracy of this article?

After the students have completed the guide sheet, the teacher facilitates a discussion of their findings about the credibility of the article and its claims. Next, the students research the claims and find evidence to support or dispute the tabloid article. The teacher supplies the students with articles from textbooks, authentic science journals (such as *Science World, Science News,* or *Scientific American*), or newspapers to help them conduct their research. Students compare and contrast the tabloid and authentic articles and create a list of characteristics for each type of writing. To summarize their findings, the class discusses how this list could be applied to other media resources such as television, radio, or the Internet.

When high school teacher Allison read the title of this article, she was a bit apprehensive about mixing tabloid articles and scientific journals. However, as she read through the article, she found that Eichinger's (2003) approach could increase conceptual understanding of a topic, initiate student motivation, and utilize reading strategies. Eichinger's activity increased conceptual understanding because the students analyzed the claims and credibility of the author. This is especially important because students are constantly being bombarded with headlines and information, as our society has become more media dependent with the advent of the Internet. The students' level of understanding would also be increased because they are identifying with the new concepts when comparing the tabloid article to the authentic journal.

Tabloid articles tend to make outrageous claims that are based upon the daily events of the world. Initially, students may find these more interesting and may then be motivated to continue to investigate the topic. Finally, during the activity, the students have a chance to practice using reading strategies such as summarizing. Students may not even realize that they are using their reading strategies because they are not reading a textbook.

To implement this practice of matching students to texts, we have to know our students. Starting this process, we *identify students' reading levels*. Guessing about this does not work effectively because some students read less well than we expect them to or than others have suggested. We use many ways to check our students' reading levels, including (1) having students read aloud, (2) asking students to write a summary of one page, (3) requesting that students write questions on a brief section of text, (4) giving a short-answer test, (5) giving a multiple-choice test, or (6) asking students to explain a text aloud. We use these informal classroom assessments with the textbook, supplementary materials, or trade books. Although oversimplified, these assessments jump-start the process of linking books to our learners.

In the end, if we truly want struggling readers to improve their reading skills, schools and teachers must take drastic measures. School districts must begin to put money into texts. By allocating funds for high-interest books and by adjusting curricula to allow for the teaching of such novels, they can take the first step in this important process. Individual teachers must recognize that it is more beneficial to have every student in a class reading a book—despite its content and reading level—than it is to teach Shakespeare's *Julius Caesar* to half of a class while the other half becomes more certain that reading is not for them.

How Self-Efficacy Develops in a Classroom: Theory and Research

In theory, self-efficacy refers to an individual's beliefs about one's capacities to learn or perform behaviors at designated levels (Bandura, 1997). Self-efficacy usually refers to performance on a task, such as kicking a soccer ball or reading a novel. It does not mean the same as "self-esteem," which is a broader sense of well-being that is not task specific. Self-efficacies can vary within an individual. For instance, one's self-efficacy may be high for soccer, but low for cooking; it may be high for reading about psychology, but low for reading about physics.

Self-efficacy is a motivational process with benefits. Following a review of research, Schunk (2003) stated, "Compared with students who doubt their learning capabilities, those who feel efficacious for learning or performing a task participate more readily, work harder, persist longer when they encounter difficulties, and achieve at a higher level" (p. 161). While low self-efficacy is often detrimental, some students perform well with moderate levels of self-efficacy. On the other hand, self-efficacy that is inappropriately high (beyond actual competencies) may lead to laziness and nonchalance. Such overconfidence may impede effort and achievement.

Students' perceptions of their performance mainly determine their levels of self-efficacy. During and after middle school, students evaluate their success on tasks. They form beliefs about their capacities by comparing to other students' progress or to their own internal standards. Higher beliefs spur higher achievement; lower ones yield losses.

To increase their self-efficacy, students benefit from observing models of excellence. When they see a difficult reading task performed well by a student or teacher, they gain information and desire. The model shows how—and thus, illustrates the steps to succeed on the task. Models also help learners form goals. The learner can see the blueprint for achievement in the form of concrete objectives to be fulfilled. The model is also motivating because the learner may think he can do as well as the person performing the task.

Research essentially suggests that students' self-efficacy can be increased through three key instructional events. First, we enable the student to set a specific goal for performing a task. The teacher or another student could provide a model of good performance. From the model, the student constructs his set of objectives. Goals can be short term (today) or long term (future). Teachers help students begin by setting short-term goals and proceeding to long-term ones. Goals can be too easy or too difficult. Obviously, the golden mean is ideal. Goals should be attainable with optimal effort and skill.

Essential to increasing self-efficacy is *feedback on progress*. As students improve, the teacher states, "You are getting better on part A or part B." The teacher does not withhold feedback until complete success occurs. It may never occur. She does not lavish the all-encompassing praise of "You are wonderful." This is too global and may not be fully accurate. Rather, she informs students about successful behaviors in reading tasks, such as, "You accurately portrayed that character," or "You thoroughly explained that math formula." Students must learn to internalize this evaluation process, giving positive and negative feedback to themselves. With well-formed internal standards and self-efficacy, students can become self-improving systems.

A study by Zimmerman and Kitsantas (2002) shows how good models and effective feedback on progress increased self-efficacy for writing. The instruction taught students how to combine simple choppy sentences into gracefully expressed thoughts. The writing strategy had five steps: (1) circle key words, (2) cross out redundant words, (3) combine key words into phrases, (4) number the phrases in importance, and (5) build the final sentence. Students gained skill and self-efficacy best when they saw a "coping model." The coping model was an example of a person doing the task well, but not perfectly. This model made mistakes, changes, and revisions, and was edited before completing the task. In contrast, the perfect model was not as helpful. Students also gained skill and self-efficacy best when they received *progress feedback* as they worked on the composition of 12 sentences. A model without feedback was not effective, and feedback without a model did not work. It is fascinating that both success in writing and belief in one's capacity to write were boosted by the same instructional elements. A range of investigations displayed the same result for reading (Schunk & Zimmerman, 1997).

Establishing Initial Confidence

When we have a text that matches our students, we give several extremely doable assignments. Especially for the wary students lacking confidence, we give short readings, easy questions, and manageable tasks. We provide quick feedback to show that they are coping well with the text. At this early point, all students are able to say, "I can read for this course." This *establishes initial confidence.*

In an effort to increase a student's self-efficacy, Fuhler (1991) explained a strategy backed by empirical research to increase student motivation in social studies classes. Fuhler suggested that social studies teachers enhance traditional textbooks with trade books related to the topic of study. For instance, when teaching the Civil War, a teacher can assign Crane's *The Red*

Badge of Courage or Cohn and Holden's *Behind Enemy Lines*, two trade books on the Civil War. Students can read the relatively easy text. They can understand the action, context, and characters quite fully. This establishes an initial confidence that they can meaningfully read historical material. This contrasts with the view that they must read textbooks to memorize and reproduce facts. Trade books complement the content by filling gaps left by the textbook. Students reading trade books were able to integrate the story into their established schema on the topic, with the overall result of increasing their knowledge. Trade books allow students to relate the topic to their own experiences. Students can connect with the characters' emotions and experiences to gain insight into their perspectives. Furthermore, such supplemental books can provide knowledge that gives students higher self-efficacy in approaching the textbook.

In social studies classes, original sources can help establish initial confidence for thinking historically, if students can relate to the writer. Original sources are actual, tangible, historic artifacts with histories of their own beyond the history they describe. In holding an authentic primary source, students are touching the past. Physical attributes of the document, such as the letterhead, color, or special markings, contribute to a primary source's ability to engage students. They also encourage critical thinking because students must evaluate the social context under which certain materials were produced and the validity and reliability of what the document says. To meet this challenge, students are intrinsically motivated to search for other documents to confirm or deny facts detailed in the originally read document. Primary sources can capture the attention of even the most reluctant readers. It is clear that students are quite interested and engaged when they are viewing actual historic documents that were produced in a time when the outcomes of these events were yet undetermined (Porter, 2003).

Setting Realistic Goals

In this instructional practice, we help students set very short-term goals for reading. We give feedback about whether their goals are met. Following success, they raise the goal slightly. Their goals may consist of fluency, answering questions, and summarizing. They are simple and text-based, and we provide feedback. Students gain *confidence through successful goal attainment.*

As stated in the theory section, self-efficacy is built on one's perception of success in reading. We provide a platform for students' self-efficacy by giving relatively simple goal setting activities at first. As oral reading fluency is a prerequisite to most forms of comprehension, we first ask students to set an oral reading goal for a text. One student may set the goal of reading one paragraph aloud with one to two mistakes, and making it sound sensible. Another student may set the goal of reading a page aloud, with no errors, and making it sound really interesting. A third student may set a goal of reading a section aloud with a partner and dramatizing the text to make it seem life-like. Students often work in partnerships at this stage.

As students meet an oral reading fluency goal, they raise the bar. They may tackle more text, harder material, longer passages, or produce higher-level rhetorical effects. Can you read well enough to make some class members feel awe, or laugh, or cry? In all, the goal is to "read to make it interesting." Reading aloud well is intimately tied to comprehension. We are not wasting our time with child's play. An eloquent reading reveals deep meanings. Oral reading and rereading increases fluency for all students, especially for poor readers, and is more vital for reading comprehension than previously believed (Archer, Gleason, & Vachon, 2003; Rasinski et al., 2005).

Sooner or later, students gain comfort in setting and meeting oral reading fluency goals with the class texts. This may take only one to two days, or it may take a month. If it drags on, we shift gears because we have selected inappropriate reading material. Given oral reading confidence, we move to simple comprehension. One technique is writing and answering questions. In pairs, students exchange questions on a short text and answer them. We arrange for them to set goals for (1) the size of the text (number of paragraphs or pages), (2) the number of questions, and (3) the difficulty of the questions (from fact finding to elaborate explanations).

Students give us their written goals, and we monitor, roughly, whether they attained them. We may grade these as pass/needs improvement to show that they count. Soon we raise the bar on goal setting by moving to summarizing. The students set goals for amount of text and length of summary. We expect this to increase. Since we cannot read all the summaries, we usually sample the class, reading about 25% and giving a grade of pass/needs improvement. Regrettably, summarizing is boring for some. However, for students who doubted their skills and feared the text, summarizing successfully is a breakthrough to self-confidence and future persistence in reading.

As students gain self-efficacy, the challenges can be enhanced. For example, as a middle school social studies teacher whose curriculum focuses on ancient civilizations, Robert uses primary sources. Robert's students read what Ramses II thought of himself (written all over his numerous monuments) or read a firsthand account of the Persian Wars (from the world's first history book by Herodotus). Students are interested to see if this information is correct and they are engaged in seeking out even more information about these people or events, and investigating the context in which they were written. Robert has found that his students are interested in reading things written thousands of years ago by someone who actually lived through the events they are discussing in class.

In this situation, Robert asks students to set small goals for which documents to read, and which historical event to relate them to. As they improve, students select longer or more challenging documents. Robert guides students to set goals for relating the documents to increasingly complex historical events. With this technique, students can set, meet, and exceed their reading goals, and thus, spiral their self-efficacy upward.

Assuring Enabling Skills

Because self-efficacy depends on successful reading, we help assure that students have three enabling skills. One is oral reading fluency. We ask the whole class, teams, partners, or even individuals to read aloud short portions of class text. Then we discuss meaning. We often reread to improve expressiveness of the oral reading. Our second enabler is linking text to knowledge. We may check each sentence, each paragraph, or each page of some texts to make the link to ourselves. Third, students need to transform text to be confident about it. When they can draw it, rewrite it, debate it, or enact it, they have changed its form. By successfully transforming the print, they build confidence in themselves as readers.

Next, we illustrate how we can link text to students' background knowledge. Many students do not believe that the text relates to them. Remote from their experience or knowledge, the text is to be memorized and forgotten. Sadly, this view stands in the way of simple comprehension because we have to connect our knowledge to every text. A simple way to get our students to learn to connect their background to text is by modeling a think-aloud. We demonstrate think-alouds by reading the text aloud as we normally would. To illustrate that even we must ask questions, we pause now and then. When students observe us asking ourselves questions, and showing a reflective demeanor, they begin to realize what it is to read. It is more than words on a page; it is one's interaction with the text that makes it real. We often think aloud about the text. For instance, during our reading of Shakespeare's *Julius Caesar*, after Brutus stabs Caesar and explains his reasons to Caesar's good friend, Mark Antony, we wonder aloud. "Wait a minute. Brutus just murdered Julius Caesar, and now he is talking to Caesar's good friend. Why would he be doing that? Why wouldn't he just kill him too? And, what does that mean: 'Not that I loved Caesar less, but that I loved Rome more.' If he loved Caesar, then why did he kill him?" At first, students will be inclined to interrupt with answers to our questions, explaining, "He wanted to do what was best for Rome." As the year goes on and we do more think-alouds, the students begin to interact more with the text. They start asking questions of the text, wondering why a character said or did something that seems contradictory. We ask the students to think aloud in pairs, teams, or as individuals, when they gain confidence. It can be slow, but students see between the lines, place themselves into the scene, and discover reading. This constant use of background knowledge is a vital enabler of reading comprehension.

In a science such as physics, creating meaning from text requires many skills. Students must be able to access the meaning of several words, integrate the meaning of individual words into sentences, and then combine the meaning of sentences into a "global meaning." This process of creating connections within a text requires students to make inferences, logical assumptions needed to make connections between sentences and paragraphs. A text's meaning often remains disjointed and detached without inferences, because texts normally do not (or cannot) state all the information relevant to the situations or events (Best, Rowe, Ozuru, & McNamara, 2005). Inferences can be generated either from earlier portions of text or from the reader's own prior knowledge.

For example, the following sentence can be found in a biology text: "The visible light is passed through the specimen and then through glass lenses" (Campbell, Reece, & Mitchell, 1999, p. 103). To understand this sentence, one must infer that the light is being passed through the microscope mentioned in the previous sentence. Without that inference, the reader might wonder for what purpose is light being passed through the specimen? Why are the lenses mentioned after the specimen? Wouldn't the light pass through the lenses first? What is a specimen? Hopefully, with the help of prior knowledge, the reader would know that a microscope uses light and lenses to magnify images. Without this information, the sentence seems to be missing a purpose. For those of us who are experienced readers, we may make inferences using our prior knowledge without even knowing it, but for students lacking in prior knowledge or of low ability, creating inferences can be a challenge when reading all literature.

To use our physics textbook effectively, we select reading passages that are just a few paragraphs long. The passages are read aloud and the class engages in a teacher-directed discussion following each paragraph. These lessons do not take a whole class period, but can address misconceptions and can actively engage students in their learning. The following example shows an in-class reading lesson on reaction energy. For students to recognize the need for inferences and to acknowledge misconceptions, we first assigned them prior knowledge activation questions regarding the topics of chemical bonds and chemical reactions, followed by a brief discussion of the answers to questions on the following passage:

> All chemical reactions are accompanied by a change in energy. Some reactions release energy to their surroundings (usually in the form of heat) and are called *exothermic*. For example, sodium and chlorine react so violently that flames can be seen as the exothermic reaction gives off heat. On the other hand, some reactions need to absorb heat from their surroundings to proceed. These reactions are called *endothermic*. A good example of an endothermic reaction is that which takes place inside of an instant cold pack. Commercial cold packs usually consist of two compounds, urea and ammonium chloride, in separate containers within a plastic bag. When the bag is bent and the inside containers are broken, the two compounds mix together and begin to react. The reaction is endothermic, absorbing heat from the surrounding environment, and the bag gets cold. (Capri, 2003, p. 1)

After reading this passage aloud, we asked the students, "What process is described using the terms *exothermic* and *endothermic*?" The initial response from most of our classes was, "Chemical reactions." Students did not initially recognize the basic relationships. To reinforce using inferences created from text, we asked students to reread the first sentence of this passage. Following this reference, students in every class were able to verbalize that exothermic and endothermic reactions describe the process of energy and heat transfer.

Then we had students use the text to define the words *exothermic* and *endothermic* to ensure that everyone understood their meanings. Students produced the definitions without any difficulty. In an effort to link students' prior knowledge regarding energy, bonding, temperature change, and chemical reactions to endothermic and exothermic reactions, we asked students to predict why there is a need for a change in energy during chemical reactions. In some cases, this question needed to be broken down into a series of smaller questions, but eventually, students used their prior knowledge to answer the question. Embedded in this passage are indications that the surrounding environment of exothermic and endothermic reactions is affected by a change in energy, but that concept is never directly written.

To highlight this concept, we proposed as our final question, "During a chemical reaction, a temperature change occurs, but at the same time, one other place is also experiencing a change in energy. What place, other than the reaction, experiences a change in energy and heat?" We follow this question with a suggestion, "To answer this question, look back to the reading.

The answer is actually present throughout the passage; it is just not clearly stated." Students had difficulty answering this question, even though the answer (the surroundings) is present in several sentences. Since the surroundings were not the main focus of any sentences in the passage, the students neglected to notice the give-and-take relationship between a chemical reaction and its environment.

Since science students are new to thinking like scientists, they are not yet trained to make connections within a system, the reaction and the surroundings jointly being the system. After rereading and discussion, students began to see the connection between the energy change of the reaction and of their surroundings. Released energy must go somewhere; if the surroundings gain energy, there must be a change in the surroundings as well as the reaction. Similarly, if the reaction absorbs energy, that energy must be taken from the environment. This change in energy causes a change in the surroundings.

We believe if left to read this passage on their own, our students would not have made the needed inferences to understand the relationship between a reaction and its environment. Thus, assuring the necessary enablement of inferences is time-intensive and demanding. However, without this scaffolding, even on-grade students will be mystified by nearly every textbook page.

Building students' self-confidence is a never-ending pursuit, a climb to Mt. Everest. It may seem impossible, or even unhealthy. But it is the journey that counts. Taking daily steps in the right direction matters just as much as a grand plan. Best, of course, is a merger of unit planning and daily action. To retrace the path blazed here, we have found success with the following instructional practices: recognizing the gap, locating student-friendly texts, establishing initial confidence, making goal setting a habit, and ensuring the enabling skills for basic reading comprehension.

6

Interest in Reading

Potency of Relevance

Robert L. Gibb and John T. Guthrie
University of Maryland

Our aim in this chapter is to talk about the benefits of supporting relevance in high school reading. What we mean by relevance is relation or connection. For every teacher, any course has its associated books, textbooks, reading materials, articles, directions, or multimedia. In large part, these are the heart of the subject matter, discipline, and topics of a course. Additionally, teachers face a multitude of students with their own personalities, wishes, and idiosyncrasies. The issue of relevance addresses the challenge of harnessing students' interests by making texts relevant.

Each individual brings a sense of *self* to the texts that represent the subject matter of the course. Students are on a quest for relevance in exploring the *me* they bring to class. They want to discover how topics and texts are useful, amusing, and purposeful in their lives. They consider topics that relate to them interesting and worthy of pursuit. Regardless of whether this is or is not a legitimate expectation, students bring these needs to every text in the classroom. In this chapter, we define relevance as the connection between the student's sense of who she is and the books or texts in courses.

The relevance of a text addresses the student's question, "How is this related to me?"

Initially we provide our view of the importance of relevance from the teacher's perspective as well as from the student's standpoint. We proceed to present our instructional handles on this slippery topic. We propose five practices that are supported in empirical research and frequently used by outstanding teachers. These instructional approaches consist of the following: *making real-world connections*, which refers to providing direct experiences for students with concrete objects and events that bring a specific feature of the subject matter to life; *personalizing with questioning*, which refers to helping students find the important and useful elements of a text through asking and answering their own questions; *extending intrinsic interests*, which consists of enabling students to gain academic skills and strategies that serve to extend their knowledge and interaction with a topic that personally appeals to them; *self-expressing*, which is the opportunity for students to display their content knowledge and expertise in the methods of the content area by using personally significant modes and media; and *puzzling*, which consists of locating and solving apparent contradictions or inconsistencies, thus penetrating beneath the surface meaning of texts. Midway through this chapter, we provide a section highlighting the research base for the practice of relevance of reading instruction at the secondary level.

Rationale for Relevance

Two major forms of relevance stand out for students and teachers alike. First, we discuss the external one, which is publicly visible: grades. For many, the most poignant part of schooling is success in the form of grades, achievement, competitiveness, test scores, and preparedness for future education. Many reading activities take relevance in this light. A particular text, consisting of a novel or a chapter in a science book, may be relevant because this reading material will be the subject of a quiz. If the quiz counts for 10% of the course grade, then this text is 10% of the student's concern in the course. A high quiz score is important because a high grade is crucial to most learners. The grade matters because the student is seeking to maximize his grade point average (GPA). The vast majority of students affirm that their GPA is a priority for themselves and their future. Thus, for these students a text takes its significance from the quiz grade and academic standing that are central to the student. If a student does not embrace the significance of grades, GPA, or future educational prospects, then the text pales, perhaps to nothing. Students with long-term lack of commitment to grades are likely to grow disaffected and drop out of school.

In this light, students read for the grade rather than for their own interest or their own understanding. It is paradoxical, however, that the actual achievement of these students is not maximized. The reason is simply that completing tasks, passing quizzes, and getting grades very imperfectly connect to content understanding. A high quiz score may show memorization more than deep comprehension. Answering 10 questions from the teacher's guide may illustrate good skills of locating specific facts but not of synthesizing broad domains of content. The most important, complex, well-integrated understandings in a discipline are hard to measure in a classroom test. This knowledge endures beyond the week after the quiz and survives as a base for learning that subject matter in the future or providing the base for a future test.

Ironically, students with the highest grade point averages are students with internal goals of reading for interest and understanding as well as reading for external goals of grades and success. The internal goals assure deeper meaning, more recall, and ultimately higher grades than the external goals only. Thus, when students are internally motivated to understand what they read, they relate new information to what they already grasp and test their knowledge with new subject matter. Therefore, it is vital for us to devote a portion of our instructional time and energy to enabling our students to fulfill their aims of finding relevance in course content. It seems sensible to emphasize relevance to internal goals (interest and understanding) as well as external goals (grades and apparent success).

Many authors have contrasted students' high interest in out-of-school literacy with their low interest in school literacy. For example, out of school, students may devote considerable time to reading and writing with their peers on line. If you ask these individuals what they read, they volunteer that they read and write messages with friends. For them, relevant literacy consists of electronically spinning the social web. In contrast, the physics textbook as an artifact of school literacy is not relevant. For many adolescents, the abyss between the two forms of literacy is wide.

We believe it is feasible to use the power of out-of-school literacy to revitalize school reading. During out-of-school reading, students are enjoying relationships or topical knowledge. They interact socially and pursue their interests. They expand their knowledge in Web site explorations. In other words, out-of-school literacy activities often link to students' knowledge, social disposition, and competencies for information seeking. Students find texts that relate to *me*, topics that connect to their knowledge, and media that follow their preferences. In these out-of-school domains, students are able to accept some texts and reject others. They form opinions and internalize beliefs because they see material as linked to them. This closely relates to our concept of *engagement,* which may occur for reading as well as out-of-school literacy (Guthrie, Wigfield, & Von Secker, 2000).

What we seek in classrooms are texts and activities that enable engagement in reading. We want to find material on physics, English, or European history that relates to students. We seek texts that connect to knowledge and beliefs that students carry with them daily. Thus, our attempt to provide relevance is an attempt to build bridges between the motivational qualities of out-of-school literacy with the content of academic curriculum. We seek the common ground between the motivations that drive students to spend hours in out-of-school literacy and the available texts that address our curriculum goals.

For some students, there are risks for engaging in school reading. If a student rejects science as a topic, he will be disinclined to read the science book. If such a student is in a peer group that disavows science because "It's not connected to me," the chasm between him and the textbook may be wide. To read the science textbook is to contradict who students say they are. For some, the internal motivators lead to a rejection of school texts, not an embrace of them. In this chapter, we are not primarily addressing students who have fine-tuned a systematic rejection of school texts. We are more often referring to students who have disconnected from text or who show apathy toward books. Students with the extreme forms of disaffection for books or hostility toward school need other principles beyond relevance (Williams, 2006).

Real-World Connection

This instructional practice refers to affording students a personal interaction with some concrete objects or events related to subject matter. Teachers think of this as hands-on activity. In a survey of middle school social studies teachers, hands-on activity was the most widely identified approach to motivating students. In helping students form a real-world connection, we seek to make a school-relevant experience as sensory as possible. We want to involve students in seeing, hearing, touching, feeling, manipulating, and interacting concretely. These experiences create interest that can be linked to books.

One of our colleagues, Suzanne, teaches sociology, an elective course for juniors and seniors. After gaining an overview of several different cultures, students select a modern culture for a research project. They must give an oral report including various aspects such as cultural values, norms, material items, and family structure. Since students often have diverse backgrounds, many opt to research the culture of their ancestors. After initially reading some self-selected texts and materials, students are expected to gather data. They may observe or interview a person who lived in that culture, such as a parent or another relative. They may read letters, view photographs, locate material objects, or hear stories about the distant culture of their informant.

Having collected data relevant to their culture, students retrieve information from encyclopedias, the Internet, and popular magazines. Finally, they give a PowerPoint presentation, create a poster, or role-play characters from the culture of their investigation. Students select criteria for an evaluation rubric for their oral reports or presentations, which gives common themes for their self-expressions. The real-world connection of interviewing, data collecting, and locating artifacts of the culture is fascinating and inspires deeper reading than is otherwise possible.

Another of our colleagues, Christopher, has successfully connected text to his students' life experiences in his on-grade level and instructionally supported middle school English classes. In teaching the book *Animal Farm* by George Orwell, difficult language such as that in Old Major's speech in chapter one was brought to life in the classroom. To accomplish this, students used markers, tape, paper plates, and scissors to create masks of animals who might have been sitting in the audience at Old Major's speech. One particular student, who was quite talented in art, made Old Major's mask for Chris to wear when he read the speech to his "constituency" (the masquerading class of animals). It helped them to grasp the chapter much better than when they read it on their own at home.

In another illustration, the benefit of real-world connections for struggling readers is evident. Any English language learners (ELLs) who are not yet proficient readers may face challenges in understanding basic science concepts such as classification. One author, Watson (2004), described a simple hands-on activity to address this issue. The scenario took place in a middle school English class, yet spans a multitude of subjects. Each student placed a shoe on the teacher's desk; then the class created a classification system for the shoes. The categories consisted of slip-on shoes, shoes with laces, shoes that buckle, and shoes with Velcro connectors. In groups, students then classified objects drawn from large lists such as candy, leaves, and clothing. Each team defended its classification system to the class, thereby gaining vocabulary and conceptual tools for discussing, critiquing, and learning classification systems. Then, the classification systems in botany or matter and energy presented in the science texts were easier to grasp and related to students' experience. Thus, the classification systems in science books became relevant because of their linkage to the real-world connection made with everyday objects, like shoes.

Real-world interactions have the ability of making facts and concepts concrete and instructive without some of the language requirements of other media. Since ELLs and struggling readers are the children who grapple with the abstractness of print, hands-on activities are a touchable route for learning that can serve to light curiosities and connect them to books. Real-world interactions, although a great source of experiential learning and fun, do not support engaged reading by themselves; they serve to arouse students' curiosity and as a launch pad to reading. When teachers supply an abundance of books on a topic to follow up on students' observations, we have seen deep student engagement in reading about that topic (Taboada, Guthrie, & McRae, in press). In fact, studies have indicated that one hour of real-world interaction can sustain 10 hours of engaged reading on a topic (Guthrie, Wigfield, et al., 2006).

The real-world activity extends to more complex laboratory experiences in science. For example, many students are confused about the relationship of weight, gravity, and speed of falling objects. They usually misunderstand the paragraphs in the physics text on this topic. Students often believe that heavy objects fall faster than light objects, but of course, they do not. One of our colleagues, Shana, said,

> Instead of presenting with a text on this topic, I refute their misconceptions by example. I climb on top of a table and hold two objects of different masses with the same surface areas and ask students to predict when each would hit the ground if released at the same time. I usually use a ping-pong ball and a foosball. Students call out their predictions prior to dropping. Most believe the heavier ball will hit first, but some guess they will land at the same time. I ask a few individuals to explain their prediction and we note their explanations on the board. I drop the balls (calling them spheres), and students witness for themselves objects falling at the same rate, regardless of mass, when air resistance is equal. Next, I ask students to predict what will happen if a heavy textbook and a piece of paper were to be dropped at the same time. I remind them that these objects have similar surface areas, but different masses. Most students predict the book will land first because it weighs more, and some add that air resistance will have a greater effect on the piece of paper. I drop the two objects and their prediction is correct, but their explanations need clarification. I next ask them to predict the rate of fall if the piece of paper was placed directly on top of the textbook. There is no change in the mass or shape of either object. I drop the object and they fall at the same rate, with the paper looking like it is glued to the book. This demonstrates that heavy objects fall faster than lighter ones, when the air resistance is the same for both objects. I help students realize air resistance and weight (a force) are two factors to consider when assessing the rate of descent for a falling object.

With these concrete observations, students gain accurate understanding of phenomena that they personally witness. Their textbook reading gains meaning as a result of this demonstration. It has specific connections to weight, mass, air resistance, and speed. Thus, as students read with deeper meaning, the text has a real-world connection for them.

Personalizing With Questioning

This instructional practice refers to the act of placing a very high premium on students' questions before, during, and throughout learning about a topic and interacting with texts on it. At the outset of nearly any topic and nearly any subject matter, students can be given a small, introductory preview or asked to describe and display their own knowledge and familiarity with a topic. Most of those students can be asked to write questions they have. These questions may help them learn, may represent true knowledge of the subject, or may be questions they would submit to the classroom pool for inclusion in a quiz. The value of the student question is that it is a personal statement; necessarily the question consists of a small portion of the total topic the student chose to attend to. The question may include the student's background information about the domain, and thus project the student's knowledge into the learning activity.

Students' questions naturally beg for answers. Students more substantially invest in reading to learn about their own question than the teacher question or the textbook question. Effective teacher probes include the following: What do you want to know? Why do you want to know that? How will that help you learn about this topic? How will that help you relate this topic to other material you know? A question is naturally relevance generating. It shows where the student currently stands in possession of facts, principles, or themes related to the topic. The question forecasts where the student could travel into the content area. A student question is a pathway into text.

In a middle school social studies class taught by our colleague Robert, students write their own questions to guide their learning about the freedoms of religion, speech, assembly, petition, and the press. They are expected to learn about the Civil War and the Constitution. The five basic freedoms are central to this unit. For some students, the questions request mere definitions, whereas for others, they reflect their interest in the historical origins or the statesmen who promoted a particular freedom. Students are expected to present a six- to eight-minute oral report about a person, event, battle, or place in the war. They write three to four questions as a way to organize the depiction of this concrete aspect of the Civil War. With teacher approval, students read and write to answer these questions as a basis for their report. Finally, students are expected to write about either a song or an invention in this time and explain its significance to the historical period. Because questions serve as the heart of an inquiry, teachers' questioning is also an important guide. When listing students' questions on the topic on the board, teachers can add their questions to give topical guidance and structural shape. Teachers' questions set models for the depth and significance of the questioning process. As a motivational teaching practice, questioning assures relevance by linking students' knowledge, interest, and preferences to the themes, topics, and persons in history. Thus, students personalize their learning and find relevance in the text.

To promote the quality of questioning as well as the motivational benefits, we recommend a rubric for questions. In this rubric, there are relatively lower and higher-level questions that can be formed on a scale of 1 (low) to 4 (high). At the bottom, Level 1 questions merely ask for a simple fact or yes/no answer. At Level 2, questions seek a simple answer to a broader concept and demand a descriptive statement. Level 3 questions contain student knowledge. These questions seek to understand an important concept, rather than a low level or trivial fact, and to probe the concept more deeply than Level 2 questions. Level 4 questions request knowledge about relationships among high-level concepts in the topic domain and a system of relationships in the subject area. For example, Level 4 questions in the social studies unit on the Civil War and the basic freedoms may ask about several different freedoms, statesmen who were responsible for them, the impact of these freedoms on social movements during the Civil War time period, and displays of these freedoms in songs or lives of individuals. Resource C presents a rubric for these questions with an example from ecological science.

Extending Intrinsic Interests

We all have things we do in our spare time. We pursue our interests purely for their own sake, not as a means to an end. For adults, intrinsic interests may be reading a novel, playing golf, doing crossword puzzles, volunteering at a homeless shelter, surfing the Internet, or writing an autobiography. Often a pursuit is inherently central to who we think we are. We are golf players or biography readers, or maybe both. By identifying an intrinsic interest in our students, we identify a key element in the self of the student that we would like to connect to subject matter in a course we are teaching. Any linkage of the self to subject matter makes the text in that subject matter relevant to the learner.

The instruction of one high school English teacher portrays a prime example of expanding intrinsic interest (Singer & Hubbard, 2002). To reach her students, who spoke a language other than English as their first language and who lived in a working class population, Singer created the *passion project*. The aim of this writing project was to identify something the student was passionate about, write on this, read about it, and explain it to others. More specifically, student directions were as follows: (1) identify a topic you are passionate about; (2) write about this topic; (3) read a novel of your choice on this topic; (4) interview someone related to this theme; (5) create a connection to your topic such as a piece of art, a trip, or a photo essay; and (6) present your topic to unveil your passion.

One student claimed that his passion was shoes. In his essay, the student stated,

> When I was in fourth grade I had a pair of camel slip-ons, no Velcro or laces. I went to the school up the street from my house with my mom and brother. The slip-ons were a little too big and whenever I kicked, they would fly into the air. I wanted to show my mom how high I could kick my shoe. I kicked it off and watched it fly through the air—going, going, gone up on the roof. My mom started to laugh, not me. I got mad at myself. The slip-ons were the only pair of shoes that I had at the time besides my sandals, so my mom and I had to go to the store and buy another pair. She said this time they had to have laces. (Singer & Hubbard, 2002, p. 331)

Indeed, this boy had a passion for shoes because he had more than 30 pairs in excellent condition, maintained in their original boxes.

In the project, the students chose a novel that connected to their personal passion.] They were taught to find books of interest to them and were amazed that novels related to their fascinations. As one student from the class concluded,

> The passion project gave us a chance to pick something we really love and dive into it in depth. We all learned something new about our passions and we all learned something about everyone else's passion. This project gave us a window into everyone in our class's mind. (Singer & Hubbard, 2002, p. 336)

Some individuals are fortunate to be passionate about reading throughout their education. We interviewed a graduate student who began early as a devoted reader. Paula first spoke of her childhood:

> I was definitely an avid reader as a child (as was my brother). The two of us used to keep flashlights hidden (or so we thought) under our pillows so we could read in bed after bedtime. I always wanted

to read the books that I saw my older brother reading so I was often reading books meant for a considerably older age level. I also enjoyed the normal young girls' series: Nancy Drew, Baby Sitters Club, etc. For some reason I loved to read the same books over and over again; in middle school I must have read *Jane Eyre* and *Little Women* twenty times apiece. By high school I was very into Kurt Vonnegut, and soon after discovered Bret Easton Ellis and Jay McInerney. These days I would consider Dave Eggers and Kurt Vonnegut as my favorite authors. I have always enjoyed reading in my free time, and believe that this love for reading as a child evolved into a love of learning in my high school years.

Paula's pursuit of her adult passion for Italian history followed:

I was fortunate to go to a university where a semester abroad was strongly encouraged, especially for history students (which, by my junior year, I was). I headed to Florence for the spring semester of my junior year without speaking more than a dozen words of Italian, and not knowing any more than the average American about Italian history or culture. Having been raised in a Jewish family, I was unfamiliar with the doctrines and traditions of the Catholic Church, which have a high degree of influence over daily life in Italy. Once there, however, I found a wonderful mentor in one of my professors. I took every class she taught, and went on day trips all over Italy with her. More than anything, she taught me to ask questions and think critically about everything I saw around me. She was a scholar primarily of medieval history, and while other students were caught up in the art and literature of the Renaissance, I discovered how fascinating—and under appreciated—the Middle Ages are. Under her tutelage, I began research that eventually became the basis for my master's thesis.

Expanding intrinsic interest cannot always be pursued on such a broad scale. It is not always possible to give such wide-open choices as the passion project or to travel to a foreign country to study. Within a unit of study, however, students will have more or less intrinsic interest in various subsections of the topic domain. The students can link an existing interest to a specific topic. Then, their understanding of the entire domain will be enhanced.

Occasionally, this may appear to be impossible. In a U.S. history course, a student may state, "My only interest is hip-hop music." A creative history teacher will affirm this student's interest in hip-hop music and ask the student to explain one hip-hop song. The teacher could then ask the student to relate this hip-hop music to one song from the Civil War. This activity may take this student (or perhaps the whole class) away from the textbook temporarily, but the detour is worth the time. The teacher may suggest that the student use information about the historical topic to compose and perform a rap. This piece on the Civil War could be presented to the class, could be taught to the entire class to present to other classes, or could even be part of an educational assembly. Many high schools and prestigious universities (e.g., Stanford University) have rap clubs and rap offs, which challenge members to create original raps on a designated topic in a designated time period. There are even competitions among schools. If students find a spark of relevance in the text, their interest, and thus their depth of reading, may increase.

When ELLs are provided opportunities to read books that relate to their cultures and mores, their cultural background and experiences become relevant to them. A portion of their lives moves to the foreground, and a connection between their interests and reading is established. As part of a middle school social studies unit, we observed students sharing their clothing, language, musical instruments, food, writing systems, and artifacts with their classmates. Students read a novel or another form of narrative from an author of their culture. They then shared their reactions to the novel with the class. Mystery, fantasy, and adventure books are genres of high interest to children. Middle school students find stories such as *Julie of the Wolves* by George and Schoenherr especially appealing. Other genres, like biographies of prominent scientists such as *John Muir: My Life with Nature* by Muir and Cornell, nicely integrate into science themes as well.

We also witnessed ELL students expressing their reading interests by creating posters, graphic organizers, diagrams, or models—all valuable forms of expressing conceptual knowledge in ways that remove some of the language burden of other types of oral presentations (Taboada, Guthrie, & McRae, in press).

One way to bring text into one's own interests is to write commentary. One teacher, Joe Oravec (2002), arranged for students to compose blogs on a Web site. They had an online diary that enabled them to write daily reflections on their school reading. In this case, these student responses were a set of shared journals in reaction to contemporary, political events in a political science course. If these journals are to be shared among students, rules and standards can be established without eradicating the students' voice in these blogs. The reactions can represent alternative perspectives, critiques, and personal opinions, but most of all, should reflect subjective reactions. Thus, students expand intrinsic interests by using them as a basis for reactions and commentary on preexisting course content. In addition, relevance is established not in the initial selection of text to be read, but in the personal positioning toward and beliefs about the text that are developed through writing and discussion in a Web site and classroom context.

How Relevance Works: Theory and Evidence

For many intuitive readers, linkage of relevance to interest is obvious, and scientific information is unnecessary to establish its credibility. Many intuitively obvious ideas, however, are incorrect. They do not stand the test of a reality check. For centuries, people intuitively believed the world was flat, but the facts turned out differently. Many people believe intuitively that heavy things fall faster than lighter ones, but all other factors being equal, they fall at the same rate. It is wise to check our intuitions whenever possible.

In the case of relevance and interest, outcomes of quantitative research are confirming. Assor, Kaplan, and Roth (2002) and Assor, Kaplan, and Kanat-Maymon (2005) found that relevance is a double-edged sword. Positive forms of relevance foster students' engagement in classroom activities and contents. On the other side, when relevance is notably missing from classroom activities and texts, students become disaffected, even to the point of experiencing such negative feelings as anger and anxiety. Evidence for these conclusions came from investigations using questionnaires with middle school students and their teachers. Students completed a questionnaire reflecting the relevance of classroom topics and activities to the outside world (Assor et al., 2002). Students who scored highly on this questionnaire experienced relevance in the classroom. These students deeply engaged in classroom activities. They participated more fully and learned more eagerly than students who did not report that the classroom seemed relevant.

The other side of this double-edged sword is equally important. Some students perceive their classrooms as nonrelevant. They view the teacher as neglecting their interests, rejecting their opinions and thoughts, interrupting their work on reading activities that were important to them, and contradicting their desire to relate their reading to their beliefs. These students who found their classes to be nonrelevant were anxious about being in the classroom and felt anger toward the teacher and the routines of the coursework. Thus, irrelevance is a negative experience with unhealthy consequences for students' commitment to reading.

In previous sections of this chapter, we described instructional practices including real-world connections and questioning as forms of personalizing. Quantitative studies that explicitly tested hypotheses have confirmed these teaching approaches. For example, students were given the hands-on experience of dissecting owl pellets in a science classroom. After classifying the bones of animals found in the owl pellet, students read about the predatory behaviors of owls and the survival processes of predators in general. In an extended curriculum unit of science and reading integration, students' motivation for reading about science topics was relatively high in comparison to other students in other curriculum units. Most important, students' reading comprehension increased more when they had a real-world connection to their texts than when they did not have this real-world association with their reading materials (Guthrie, Wigfield, et al., 2006).

Helping students find relevance through questioning and pursuing their questions as educational goals is also associated with motivation and achievement. Students who are adept at asking high-level questions are typically more motivated for reading than students who are less competent in the questioning process (Tonks, Taboada, Wigfield, & Guthrie, 2007). This confirms that curiosity is a quality that enables learners to display their keenness for learning as well as their aptitude for investigating subjects effectively. In other words, students with good inquiry and questioning skills are most often motivated learners. When we provide high-level questions and encourage our students to ask questions that demand deep explanations and patterns of evidence, we create higher engagement in learning than if we ask lower level questions. In turn, because achievement in reading responds to motivation for reading, asking and encouraging high-level questioning tends to enable students to grow in reading more effectively (Taylor, Pearson, & Peterson, 2003).

Many forms of evidence can be marshaled to document the linkage of relevance and interest. For example, relevant topics are familiar to us. A relevant topic is one we have encountered before and learned something about. Not surprisingly, familiar topics are interesting (Alexander, Jetton, & Kulikowich, 1995). All other things being equal, if we see a book, a movie, or a person who is familiar, we are more likely to find this encounter to be more interesting than if it is unfamiliar. While some encounters (e.g., some people we meet) are unpleasant and uninteresting, in general, the trend holds. The reason the trend holds is that the unfamiliar book or topic is inherently uninteresting. If we know absolutely nothing about a topic (e.g., how microwaves move), it is extremely rare that we find the topic arresting. In conclusion, relevant things are familiar, and familiar things are interesting, thus confirming the linkage of relevance and interest.

An explanation for this association is not so obvious. How do relevant topics motivate us? It is self-evident that people enjoy exercising their beliefs. They work to fulfill their values, pursue their favorite recreations, and accomplish their self-set goals. They learn easily about favorite topics, whether this learning is through print medium or otherwise.

A relevant text connects to that person's sense of self. It relates to who she believes she is. Consequently, a relevant text is enabling. It helps the individual attain her goals. It fosters her enjoyment of favorite activities. Conversely, a nonrelevant text carries the opposite qualities. It is unrelated to her interests, and consequently, is comparatively insignificant.

By definition, the individual does not know about the content of a nonrelevant text. Yet in a school situation, students are constantly expected to understand unrelated things. The learner, however, has no inherent, *internal* reason for this understanding. Without special teacher support, there is no internal reason for reading the nonrelevant text.

A relevant text is essentially a bridge between the individual and his potential. Because the relevant text is slightly familiar, its topic is slightly known. The content is slightly understood before reading. There is an overlap between the knowledge of the reader and the content of the text. Because the individual is in a constant state of exercising his interests, the text is a bridge to potential knowledge and beliefs. The same cannot be said of a nonrelevant text. This unrelated reading material is a bridge that goes nowhere. As a result, the nonrelevant text has a low likelihood of helping the individual fulfill his potentialities.

Self-Expression

Reading in secondary school is a two-way street. On one side is a text to be absorbed, and on the other side is a student display of knowledge about the text. Although we can only sample minute quantities of the actual knowledge that students gain, those samples are vitally important. These samples of student knowledge are also vital because they impact the students' experience of text relevance (Werderich, 2002). If our sample of student knowledge (quizzes and grades) is based, for example, on short-answer questions, the student enters a mode of reproducing bits of text. The sense of self never enters the picture. In this circumstance, the text is not relevant in the student's eyes. We have seen the disastrous effects of students' continued and repeated experience with nonrelevant texts. Consequently, it is our goal as educators to make text relevant through self-expression.

When a student writes his own PowerPoint about an historical era, composes his own essay about a novel, creates a political cartoon, or designs her own experiment in biology, the student makes a self-statement. This self-expression of content knowledge, based on course texts and other learning, represents a link between the text and the self of the student. By choosing the topic, the medium, or the hypothesis, the student exercises his beliefs about what is important. His values can come into play, however slightly. The act of linking text to self brings interest into the classroom.

Teachers are adept at creating a spectrum of opportunities for self-expression. In the professional literature in English, science, history, and mathematics, as well as in classrooms in every state, we are creating relevance through encouraging student self-expression. Examples include making a multimedia PowerPoint about an historical event, constructing an essay from the viewpoint of one character in a novel, making a poster to display a science experiment, writing a speech from the perspective of a statesman, and composing word problems in mathematics that illustrate the use of a certain formula.

These forms of self-expression can bring relevance to texts at many levels within a course of study. For instance, knowledge about an entire four-week unit might be captured by students' work on a PowerPoint presentation, video, or play composed to show the genre of the time period. More important, we need not wait until the end of the unit to invite such self-expression. For example, a section of text could be the basis for students to display their knowledge according to their own likes. In science, students could be asked to pose a concept map of a three-page section of the textbook. Most often, there is more than one legitimate concept map that will represent the text, more than one organizational framework, and more than one set of key words that are valid representations of text meaning. Consequently, students' selection of words, organizational perceptions, and previous understandings come into play as they draw this concept map. In history, a brief, three-page section of the textbook could become the basis for identifying a character, finding out enough to write one paragraph, and sharing this paragraph with a team or class. Learning becomes a self-expression.

Even at the level of one page, we can invite self-expression. In any subject, we may take one page and ask students to identify the six most important words. As previously indicated, there may be more than one set of valid key terms, and students can be asked to argue for their list or their configuration of these words in a spatial diagram. The selection, organization, and argumentation that may accompany the simple activity are relevance generating.

In a previous chapter, we discussed mastery goals, which lead to understanding text beneath its surface level. For us and our students, mastery goals are connected with words like explaining, debating, persuading, exemplifying, illustrating, and arguing. If a student is doing one of these things based on her understanding of a page, section, or unit of text, she is expressing herself. She brings her personal knowledge, perspective, and values into play in these displays of understanding. Self-expressions, then, are links of self to text. Consequently, they induce interest in reading (Bintz & Shelton, 2004; Bitz, 2004).

Puzzling

In this practice, teachers encourage students in finding and composing puzzles related to their texts. Puzzling may include locating the contradiction in a book. In a novel, history book, and even science texts, there may be information that seems to conflict with itself. A diagram may conflict with a paragraph. One character in a story may behave in contradictory ways in different scenes. These are puzzles to be identified and sorted out.

Puzzling may also include posing problems. For example, in a unit on ecology, students may learn about global warming and may ask, "How much warming needs to occur for the cities of Los Angeles, New Orleans, and New York to become flooded?" Students pose this problem that could easily merit further reading and debate. The process of puzzling may include taking new perspectives. Especially powerful in history or literature, many texts are now available to foster this process. For example, Jane Yolen's book *Encounter* is a story of Christopher Columbus's discovery of San Salvador told from the viewpoint of a young islander. This boy recounts the tale as an old man warning his neighbors about the dangers of the uninvited guests. This new perspective may be presented as a puzzle in the context of Columbus's discovery of the new world. Likewise, in a unit on Civil War history, students might read letters from soldiers that place the diplomacy of North and South into a different context.

To describe and understand a political event and the people contributing to it, students could write political cartoons that represent puzzles. A drawing may give one meaning and the caption may be a surprise or may introduce a paradox. This composition of a political puzzle clearly demands text-based understanding of people, events, and their interpretations (Ciardiello, 2003; McLaughlin & DeVoogd, 2004).

In science, students can find or compose puzzles related to applications of basic ideas. In learning about photosynthesis, students can write questions beginning with "Imagine if." For example, in learning about the dependence of plants on sunlight, students might pose, "Imagine if plants could grow without sun." What would be the results and implications? Students studying the science of ecology examining an ant colony may ask, "Imagine if the life cycle of the ant colony is disrupted; what happens to the trees and birds that depend on the ants in various ways?" To address these puzzles and solve them, students need to read, debate, write, or utilize their collaborative reasoning. In any case, their reading activities will link to a puzzle of their making. This will usher in a slight, or even profound, fusion of text and self, and thus, a motivation for extended comprehension.

7

Growing Motivation

How Students Develop

John T. Guthrie
University of Maryland

Teachers share a common meaning for motivation. When we talk about motivation we refer to students' interests, desire to learn, and commitment toward reading. Beyond that, many teachers report the following beliefs:

- Students come to my class either well motivated or not motivated.
- Parents are mostly responsible for students' dedication to school.
- Motivation comes and goes unpredictably.
- We have to teach for achievement, and motivation is a luxury.
- There is usually not too much I can do to influence motivation.

Although these beliefs are valid, there is also a flip side. A reality check from research shows that teachers often influence students' motivations, within limits.

In this chapter we review theory and evidence that point toward seven key principles about classroom motivation: (1) *context counts* because the specific books or teacher actions in the classroom influence motivation; (2) *situated motivation is significant* because interest develops with a very concrete, immediate beginning; (3) *motives move from outside to inside the learner,* and therefore, the teacher plays a potentially substantial role as an outsider who influences development; (4) *internal motivation drives achievement,* which contradicts the widespread belief that it is the grade, prize, or reward that powers students' academic accomplishment; (5) *students' general motivation for school reading is stable,* showing that interests students develop will last over time; (6) *internal motivation declines,* which raises the bar for the importance of teacher and school support for students' motivational development; and (7) *cause and effect between motivation and achievement are interconnected,* but motivation becomes the driver as students advance in school. This chapter presents and comments about research pertinent to each of these points.

Context Counts

Ask nearly any student the question, "Do you have a favorite book?" After a moment or two he may come up with a title or an author. Even students who claim they do not read or do not like to read often recall one book that was delightful or important (Guthrie et al., in press). Likewise, if you ask young adults what influenced their education, they overwhelmingly mention a favorite teacher. This teacher believed in them, inspired them, or encouraged them to pursue an interest. Persons with this memory of a favorite teacher usually were more successful in school than individuals who draw a blank to this question (Ruddell, 1995).

So far in this book we have talked about how specific teacher actions influence students' motivations. In an earlier chapter, we mentioned how mastery goals (e.g., Let's understand this material) are much more energizing in the long run than performance goals (e.g., Let's pass this test). Likewise, when we arrange for a particular choice that is appropriate for a specific lesson, student motivation and reading for that lesson, and perhaps for that topic, clearly increase. When we arrange for students to collaborate, the text becomes more interesting than a text that students must assimilate in isolation. Because the context of a classroom is composed of its books, teachers, teacher actions, and student behaviors, we see that context does count for motivation. Although the drive to read is partly located within the learner, it is also significantly driven by the context, which is under our control.

Context impacts motivations in two directions, both upward and downward. As Assor and colleagues (Assor, Kaplan, & Roth, 2002; Assor, Kaplan, & Kanat-Maymon, 2005) illustrated, students became more interested and engaged in classroom activities when teachers made the content of the reading activities interesting and provided meaningful choices. Conversely, student interests and commitments to reading activities are also reduced and depressed by some teacher actions. For example, teachers can be too controlling. If we frequently start and stop students in specific activities during a 45-minute period, students feel coerced. If we interrupt students when they are reading, writing, thinking, or talking about something that they value, they feel that their interests are discounted. This practice of overcontrol may lead to anger. Under these conditions, students get mad at us or at their peers, and they may strike out verbally or behaviorally.

Over time during the school year, the context has a spiraling effect on students' engagement. At the beginning of the year, if we provide support for students' engagement in reading, students' motivation increases. As students become more participatory, responsible, and self-directing in their learning, we afford more motivational support through wider choices, longer collaborations, and more interesting learning activities. Thus, the positive spiral moves upward.

The negative spiral can move downward. At the beginning of the school year, if we are controlling to the point of suffocation, overly directive, and constraining, students respond with resistance. Their objections may be passive in the form of not reading their homework or reading superficially. Resistance may also express itself as vocal objections, arguments, or insults in a classroom. Faced with this behavior, we may introduce punishments, sanctions, and real threats. For all but an extreme minority of students, our classrooms will become an unpleasant place to be. For most students, an interest in content and commitment to learning will decline, obviously reducing achievement (Skinner & Belmont, 1993).

It is fascinating that the context formed by teacher actions in a 20-minute activity will influence students' motivation, engagement, and success in performance. Reeve and Jang (2006) conducted an investigation with preservice teachers who were being trained to provide engaging instruction. With 72 pairs of teachers, one person took the role of an instructor who taught the other person about a puzzle. Those participating as the students reported their engagement in the learning activity including their attention, effort, persistence, verbal participation, and positive emotion. Outside raters observed the teachers' actions to record the autonomy support provided by the teachers. Teachers' highly engaging actions were positively related to student enthusiasm, perceived autonomy, and successful performance with the puzzle. These actions included the following: (1) time spent listening, (2) asking what the student wants, (3) time allowing the student to work in his own way, (4) time the student is talking, (5) seating arrangements, (6) providing rationales, (7) praising informational feedback, (8) offering encouragement, (9) offering hints, (10) being responsive to student questions, and (11) communicating perspective-taking statements. Teachers who did more of these instructional behaviors had students who were more interested, engaged, and successful than other teachers.

Conversely, several instructional behaviors had negative effects. Each of the following behaviors was associated with decreased perceived autonomy, engagement, and success in working with the puzzle: (1) time holding the learning materials, (2) exhibiting solutions, (3) uttering answers, (4) giving directives or commands, (5) making "should" statements, and (6) asking controlling questions. These negatively affected students' perceived autonomy, which was their feeling that they were doing what they decided to do, that they had choices, and that they felt free to adopt new approaches. These teacher actions in this brief, 20-minute period also depressed the engagement and reduced puzzle-solving success. Thus, context counts in solving a puzzle, reading a given book on a given day, and becoming engaged in a course. Although students bring motivations to the classroom and parents inevitably influence their children's commitments, classroom context makes a systematic impact on students' growth in engagement (Reeve & Jang, 2006).

Situated Motivation Is Significant

As you may have noticed, there is an apparent paradox when we talk about how context influences motivation. On one hand, research confirms that students come to a given class with a certain level of motivation. For some students it is high; for some it is low. Yet at the same time, we have seen that nearly everyone has a favorite book. Likewise, a specific classroom activity may be interesting to everyone.

This paradox can be resolved by seeing motivation in two ways: motivation may be either general or situational. General motivation is a broad trait that endures across time and appears in a variety of circumstances. For example, a student may have generally high self-efficacy for school. She may be confident in English, science, and history. She may approach reading, writing, and class discussion activities with a sense that she can succeed well in them. This is generalized self-efficacy for school.

In contrast, a situational motivation refers to a particular circumstance. For example, a boy with situational self-efficacy may be confident that he can succeed in reading a section of a specific book at a given point in time. He knows he can handle this reading task. However, this boy may not believe he is a good reader in general. He may even believe he is a poor reader for certain books such as science texts. Thus, self-efficacy can be situated to a particular text at a point in time.

The situational qualities of motivation have been studied with respect to interest. Hidi and Renninger (2006) summarized more than 150 studies showing that interest develops from the specific to the more general. Guthrie, Wagner, Wigfield, Tonks, and Perencevich (2006) recorded many of these changes specifically for reading. According to these authors, there are four stages in interest development. First, the initial spark of any long-term interest is a particular circumstance, consisting of a single text in a unique situation with one or more persons in a spot like home. The student shows an interest in this milieu. He may smile, talk, or read with enthusiasm. However, the interest is limited to the particular event and the activity the student wants to perform with reading.

The second stage is shown by a person who has a focus, attention, and persistence over a text during an extended period of time for a narrow type of reading. Her reading may occur on several occasions, perhaps with encouragement from another person such as a peer or teacher. However, the interest is limited to one topic and one type of reading material. For example, three girls may avidly read two to three celebrity magazines that they frequently talk about, and this may encourage more reading and learning in their favored domain. Although it exists across time and a set of magazines, their interest focuses on this topic and these reading materials.

At the third stage, students seek repeated opportunities to read about a topic over an extended time period, and the person may gain substantial amounts of knowledge and value from this reading activity. Topics they read about may subdivide and deepen, although focus may be maintained. For example, the girls' fascination with celebrities may expand to their histories, including a wide range of well-known individuals about whom these girls gain full understanding and acquire positive feelings. More frequently, a well-developed interest at this level would include a topic such as animal survival, ancient Greek history, or American literature. A student who reads about one of these domains gains the webs of information and powers of discrimination that represent strongly developed and substantially focused interest.

At the fourth and last stage of interest development, individuals display substantial knowledge, high values for reading and learning, and complex strategies for digging deeply into a topic. Individuals at this level are likely to create their own interests and generate new curiosities, rather than being dependent upon other persons or environmental pushes to expand their reading and information. Examples may include an individual who pursued ecology professionally and personally, an astronomer who read widely and frequently, or a person fascinated with the political science of Eastern nations such as China. Such a person may read, at many different times and in a range of locations, a diverse array of books, materials, Web sites, magazines, and media, sharing these with others whenever possible.

The way reading develops is that it begins simply. That is why situated motivation is significant. If the spark is fanned by positive response and by others' encouragement, interest may grow. The process of generalization consists of the spreading into new subtopics, diverse materials, and a broader community of interchange. It may end in highly creative thinking, writing, and the development of expertise (Guthrie, Wigfield, et al., 2006).

Some adults who are avid readers and high achievers began with disabilities. Reading did not come naturally and well, but with burning motivation, they gained a focus of interest and entered the world of readership. One investigator who has studied dozens of these individuals reported on one who became a prominent professor (Fink, 1992). One of her cases was Ron, who began creative, scientific experimentation during the elementary grades. He said, "I started to experiment with chemistry. I set up a lab in the basement and then needed to get supplies. So I set up a fake company, got letterhead printed, and then basically started ordering things through chemical supply companies. That early experience was useful, building your own confidence by doing these things" (Fink, 1992, p. 172).

To pursue this fascination with chemistry, Ron continued by saying,

> You start reading a lot. Because you like it, you read science for how things are put together. My interest in chemistry just came...it started with my interest in airplanes in grade school...that quickly converted to propellant systems in seventh and eighth grades. So the way to understand that was to start reading chemistry books. I became fascinated with nitrogen chemistry so I got organic chemistry textbooks. I read quite a few college texts when I was a high school freshman." (Fink, 1992, p. 175)

Ron was not a reader in general and many of his classes were challenging. He stated,

> I failed an English class in college. I got an F. I could never do English. In my high school, they (English teachers) passed me. But basically in high school, if you attend the class, and you do the assignments, even with Fs, you pass. I didn't do very well in History, but I passed. I spent time trying to memorize it and regurgitate it back to the teacher. (Fink, 1992, p. 176)

As this investigation shows, this struggling reader gained an intense interest in chemistry and succeeded highly in this subject domain. However, in the noninterest domains, such as English and social studies, he was low in achievement and partially succeeded by sheer perseverance. According to Fink (1992), the key elements that contributed to these students' development of reading consisted of the following: (1) an area of intense personal interest, (2) avid reading about this discipline, and (3) the development of deep knowledge in this domain. From situational motivation in a topic, these individuals developed into avid readers in a discipline.

Motives Move From Outside to Inside

A motivation for doing something can be relatively more inside of you (internal) or relatively more outside of you (external). Consider these questions. You might ask a student, "Why do you read?" (You could ask yourself this same question.) The answers of your student could range from internal to external. Answers could also be negative. Following is a rank order from internal to external to negative reasons for reading:

- Because I experience enjoyment reading new things (intrinsic motivation)
- Because I value reading and its benefits (identified motivation)
- Because I want to succeed in my studies (introjected motivation)
- To get better grades (external motivation)
- I cannot see why I read and frankly I couldn't care less (amotivation)
- I dislike school reading and avoid it (resistance motivation)

These are very different reasons for reading. The significance of these different reasons is that the most internalized reason (pleasure and satisfaction in reading) is connected to things we value such as school achievement, a sense of well-being, and school adjustment. On the other side, the most negative of these motivations refers to resistance and avoidance. When this motivation sets in, chances of dropping out of school rise dramatically. It is not primarily whether a student reads or not, but rather the reasons for that reading, that determine these important outcomes. Motivations are presented in Table 7.1, along with their designation as internal or external, and the key qualities that characterize them.

Table 7.1   Motivations for Reading

Locus	Motivation	Quality of Reading
Internal	Intrinsic	Enjoyment
Internal	Identified	Ownership
External	Introjected	Success
External	External	Grade
Demotivation	Amotivation	Apathy
Demotivation	Resistance	Avoidance

These reasons for reading have been coordinated into a framework named *self-determination theory*, conceptualized by Deci and Ryan (1985). According to this theory, there are many different reasons why an individual engages in a specific type of behavior or action. Underlying attitudes and goals that give rise to the action are vitally important. Intrinsic motivation refers to doing something for its own sake, such as playing golf, chatting socially, or reading. However, not all behaviors are inspired by intrinsic motivation. Although most of us would be grateful if our students were intrinsically motivated to do the work and if they enjoyed the activities that we planned on a regular basis, it is unrealistic to assume this is always the case (Ryan & Deci, 2000a).

Much student reading is prompted by external factors such as grades or other rewards. These factors are known as *external motivation*. According to Ryan and Deci (2000b), students acquire motivation through a process known as *internalization* or *integration of values*. This development is explained as taking a value or goal from a significant other such as a parent or teacher, and slowly internalizing it into one's self. Even within a classroom in a short period of time, students can internalize a teacher's positive value for reading engagement and get more involved in learning for a course (Reeve, Jang, Carrell, Jeon, & Barch, 2004).

Four levels of positive motivation exist. They differ in how internal and external they are. At the external levels, someone else gives the individual the reason for reading. At the internal levels, the individual gives herself the reason for reading. In order of lowest to highest based on amount of internalization these motivations are (1) external, (2) introjection, (3) identification, and (4) intrinsic.

External motivations consist of trying to gain reward and avoid punishment. A child who reads for homework to avoid being punished is an example of being externally motivated. These students just memorize material presented to them by the teacher. Without critically processing the information, students are unable to connect it with their prior knowledge, therefore prohibiting themselves from having a deeper understanding of the material (Rozendaal, Minnaert, & Boekaerts, 2005).

The next level of external motivation is introjected. Students with this type of motivation may read to gain success, in the form of recognition. However, they do not value reading personally or take ownership of school reading. They tend to feel very controlled because they read to avoid guilt or anxiety. This level of motivation is initiated by an external force (Ryan & Deci, 2000b).

The last two levels, identified and intrinsic motivations, are what we are striving to reach with our students. These are internal motivations. At this end of the spectrum, students have realized the value of reading and have internalized it as part of who they are. A student with an identified motivation values reading and sees its benefit for herself and her future. For example, a student may realize it is important to do well in science. She will focus, not because she is forced by a teacher or parent, but because she understands the importance of success in science to ultimately achieve her goals.

Students who are intrinsically motivated enjoy reading. They have favorite topics, authors, or series of books. Individuals with intrinsic motivations have a positive sense of well-being because their basic psychological needs for autonomy, competence, and relatedness are being met. Therefore, students who are more intrinsically motivated tend to enjoy school and are better able to handle difficult situations (Sheldon, Elliot, Kim, & Kasser, 2001).

It is valuable for students to be on the internalized end of the spectrum. These students exhibit more successful behaviors than students who only do things because they feel it is necessary for an external reward. Students who have identified or intrinsic motivation tend to have greater engagement (Connell & Wellborn, 1991), better performance (Miserandino, 1996), a lower dropout rate (Vallerand & Bissonnette, 1992), and a higher quality of learning (Grolnick & Ryan, 1987) than other students. Kasser and Ryan (1993, 1996) found that these types of motivations can improve students' mental health.

Alternatively, students who are more motivated by external rewards tend to be less interested in schoolwork, do not put forth as much effort, and tend to blame others such as their teachers when they are not successful. Many researchers try to explain the negative effects of being driven by external rewards. One explanation is that individuals who attempt to achieve goals for external rewards such as grades, money, or fame are often not receiving fulfillment of basic psychological needs. Instead, these individuals are focused on social comparisons to enable them to determine their level of success. They do not have an internal standard for success and satisfaction, but rely excessively on other individuals for their gratification.

The progression of motivations from outside (external) to inside (internal) is most obvious for reading in early childhood. Children are not born into this world with an interest in reading. Most often, a parent reads with a child, suggesting that a book reading activity may be fun, pleasurable, and valued. Thus, the goal of reading well and reading for enjoyment may begin with the parent and may slowly be absorbed by the child until the child self-initiates reading activities. External forces that drive reading may include teachers, peers, and the culture that values gaining knowledge, which is often accessible through printed resources. The process of internalizing the goals, behaviors, and values of reading may occur continually from preschool through high school. A high school student may certainly follow the suggestion of a respected teacher to read about a certain poet or a given historical figure. If this sparks the development of interest, it is an example of a motive moving from outside to inside.

Among high school students, investigators have shown that the process of internalizing motivations for academic work is occurring continually. One demonstration reported by Otis, Grouzet, and Pelletier (2005) for 646 students in Grades 8 to 10 showed that there was a *domino effect* for motivations from the more external to the more internal. The rank order of motivations from most external to most internal (listed at the beginning of this section) consisted of the following: external, introjected, identified, and intrinsic. When students develop from more external to more internal, we can expect that the correlations among the relations will increase from lower to higher on this scale of internalization.

Students who are high on an external motivation scale will also be high on an introjected scale of motivation. However, these students may not be very high in intrinsic motivation. Therefore, the correlation between external and introjected is higher than the correlation between external and intrinsic for these eighth- to tenth-grade students. Likewise at the other end, the correlation between intrinsic and identified is higher than the correlation between intrinsic and external. Called a *simplex pattern*, this finding suggests that students' growth in motivation follows the external to internal sequence.

Two important implications of this process of internalization are significant. First, we should not assume that motivation is not inborn. Just as physical stature and knowledge advance, motivations grow during high school. The second implication is that it is disastrous for students to get stuck in a completely external form of motivation for reading. When students cease to move beyond external motivation, they severely delimit their futures.

Internal Motivation Drives Achivement

Overwhelmingly, students report that they will study, read, participate in class, or write about the subject matter to get a good grade. As a goal for the homework, quiz, test, or course, the final grade is paramount. External motivators such as grades can control behavior and attention. A teacher in a 10th-grade class can immediately command focused attention from all students by saying, "This material will be on the test." This same teacher can produce quiet in an unruly classroom by saying, "If this class is not silent, we will have a quiz now." A teacher will gain strict conformity in this classroom by stating, "Any student who interrupts in the next 10 minutes will lose five points." These external motivators have strong and immediate effects.

As tools for crisis intervention, we often find external motivators to be necessary. However, the paradox is that external motivation does not determine students' achievement on tests or their academic success in a course or in school as much as internal motivation does. Surprising as it may seem, students who are driven only by their grades are not necessarily higher achievers than students who are much less grade driven. The motives that drive students toward academic achievement are not grades, rules, and teacher commands. This is a bit counterintuitive, and we will unpackage it.

Several studies report a lack of connection between external motivators and academic achievement in reading. For example, Otis et al. (2005) showed that for eighth- to tenth-grade students, grades (external) and competition for recognition (introjected) were not correlated with success in homework. Students with a high grade-oriented motivation were not more likely to successfully do the reading and writing for homework across subject matters than students with lower grade-oriented motivations were. In a study of approximately 2000 middle school students in grades six to eight, external (extrinsic) motivations were generally unrelated to achievement (Unrau & Schlackman, 2006). An almost identical finding was observed by Wang and Guthrie (2004) for both Caucasian and Asian elementary school students. Extrinsic motivation was not related to test scores in reading. Thus, external drivers, shockingly, do not consistently increase reading achievement.

The other side of the coin is surprising and consistent. Internal motivation spurs a wide range of engagements in reading (Fredericks, Blumenfeld, & Paris, 2004). By internal motivators, we include two major qualities of the learner-intrinsic motivation and identified motivation. Otis et al. (2005) showed that both of these qualities were associated with doing homework and participating in school. In the investigation by Unrau and Schlackman (2006), these intrinsic motivations predicted standardized test scores in reading achievement for students in grades six to eight. Intrinsic motivation worked for all students, irrespective of their grade level or gender. For students in the later elementary grades, Wang and Guthrie (2004) reported this powerful correlation of intrinsic motivation and tested reading achievement, even when previous grades were statistically controlled. There are many forms of evidence for this principle. Most convincing, Vansteenkiste, Lens, and Deci (2006) conducted experiments showing that when internal motivators guide reading, students understand deeply and conceptually. On the other hand, when external motivators guide reading, students only gain the surface meaning. This is important because it shows that changes in achievement within a school year are driven by internal motivation. At the same time, those changes are not influenced by external motivators of grades or competition (Mac Iver, Stipek, & Daniels, 1991; Skinner, Wellborn, & Connell, 1990).

To get a closer feel for the internal motivation of middle school students, Dowson and McInerney (2003) interviewed 86 students and observed them in their middle school setting. The internally motivated students reported, "I like learning new topics, even if they're hard, because they're interesting rather than just repeating things over and over." These students enjoyed challenging academic work, despite its difficulty. They commented, "When I'm interested in what the teacher asks us to write, I think about how I'm going to do it before I start." In other words, these students planned their reading and writing and used strategies to attain their high goals. Likewise, students who identified with the school goals for reading gained satisfaction, even though they did not enjoy the content. They planned their courses in concert with teachers and parents to achieve highly and work toward long-term goals.

In contrast, the students who were amotivated said, "I don't care whether I understand it or not. I just know that I will get a good grade if I copy what the teacher writes." Regrettably, students reported, "I get so stressed about schoolwork that I don't even want to do what I have to do." Too many students feel anxious to the point where engagement in schoolwork becomes difficult. When the desire for grades and competitiveness generates anxiety, negative effects on achievement are inevitable.

General Motivation Is Stable

We have talked about the power of context to impact students' motivations for reading. However, we said that those positive influences occur for *situated* motivation. A feature of the context, such as a teacher's enthusiasm about reading a particular book, may very likely enhance students' situational interest in that book at that time on a temporary basis. However, general motivation, rather than being sensitive to context and changeable, is quite stable. By general motivation, we refer to the enduring motivation with staying power.

From one year to the next, general motivation tends to remain consistent. For example, a student may enter ninth grade with an accumulation of failures and disappointments that have led to amotivation. This student does not care about reading in any course. To measure global motivation, researchers use questionnaire items such as the following: "I often find it interesting to read about topics in school." Students who report that they "strongly agree" with this at the end of eighth grade are likely to report that they strongly agree with this statement at the end of ninth grade as well. In parallel, eighth-grade students who report, "This statement is not at all true of me" will likely sustain that report in ninth and 10th grades.

This stability has shown to hold from ages 9 to 17 in a study of 115 students by A. E. Gottfried, Fleming, and A. W. Gottfried (2001). They looked at reading in English, social studies, history, and science in middle and high schools. Students reported their levels of enjoyment and satisfaction from reading in these contents areas, which provided a quantitative scale of internal motivation for reading and learning from text. From ages 13 to 17, the correlation of intrinsic motivation from one time to the next was .72. This statistic implies that half of the differences between students (age 17 and older in high school) were determined by the motivation of students at age 13 (as they entered middle school). This is a high amount of stability compared to mathematics. In math, correlation of motivation between ages 13 and 17 was .22. This signifies that less than 5% of the differences between 17-year-olds were attributable to their motivation at age 13. So the backdrop of motivational stability for reading is quite strong. If context is going to impact reading motivation, then this set of school and teacher inputs into context should be strong and sustained. These findings of stability across time were confirmed for eighth to tenth graders by Otis et al. (2005) and for sixth to eighth graders by Unrau and Schlackman (2006).

Global Internal Motivation Declines Across Time

There is an apparent contradiction that even though general motivation is stable, it declines slowly across time. If you ask students, "How much do you like to read?" the positive answers will be relatively high in elementary school. In second and third grades, the reply is generally, "I like to read a lot!" From about Grade 4 onward, the reply declines. We found in Grade 4 that about 75% of students will agree with the statement, "I think reading is interesting." By Grade 8, about 67% of students have reversed. In contrast, they agree with the statement, "I think reading is boring." From elementary to middle schools, reading degrades from interesting to boring. In a longitudinal study with the same students across time, A. E. Gottfried et al. (2001) showed that internal motivation for reading decreased from ages 9 to 10, 10 to 13, and 13 to 16, and stayed about the same from ages 16 to 17. Declines in motivation were consistent into high school. The drop was approximately 7% from ages 9 to 17 in this study. However, a different investigation showed that the drop in internal motivation from grades seven to eight was approximately 7%. Although the decrease is consistently reported, the amount of decrease is not easy to compare across studies because different questionnaires are used and none of the scales have a real starting score of zero because no one actually knows what "zero" motivation is.

Although the decline of internal motivation in reading is repeated in many studies, not everything declines. For example, in A. E. Gottfried's (1985) longitudinal investigation, students' interest in social studies and history did not change from ages 9 to 17, nor did their global interest in school in general. Also, students' interest in sports did not drop from the elementary grades to middle school. In comparison, students' interest in performing music declined more precipitously from elementary to middle school than their interest in reading or math (Wigfield, Eccles, Mac Iver, Reuman, & Midgley, 1991).

Recent evidence also shows that external motivation declines during the middle and high school years. Looking at external motivators of grades, competition, recognition, and compliance with school rules, Unrau and Schlackman (2006) found decreases from Grades 6 to 7 and 7 to 8. These decreases occurred for girls as well as boys, including Hispanics and Asians. Adding weight to the evidence, Otis, Grouzet, and Pelletier (2005) showed that intrinsic motivation for studying declined from Grades 8 to 9 and 9 to 10. Furthermore, the value of recognition and competition (introjected motivation) declined from eighth to ninth grades and ninth to tenth grades. Likewise, the students' view of the importance of grades and future salary dropped from eighth to ninth grades and ninth to tenth grades as well. So the external motivators are declining in level of importance, although not as markedly as the internal motivators (Otis et al., 2005).

Some of what we may have stated in the last section of this chapter may seem contradictory. For example, we claimed in the previous section that internal motivation was stable. In this section we stated that internal motivation declines. Do these statements conflict? In fact, they do not. The stability refers to the rank order of individuals in a large sample. For example, if Stephen is number 10 out of 500 and Alicia is number 80 out of 500, Stephen is higher than Alicia. In the next year, if Stephen is number 15 and Alicia is number 90, Stephen is still higher than Alicia. Their relative positions in the rank ordering have not altered. Their absolute scores (the real ones) may have both decreased, but their relative scores (compared to the total sample) have remained quite similar. Thus, we can have stability in relative scores and a decline in absolute scores at the same time.

Another possible confusion may arise from the dual facts that internal motivation drives achievement, yet internal motivation declines over time. Does this mean that motivation should decline over time? Not necessarily. The correlation of internal motivation and achievement is based on relative data. The student who is more highly motivated than others tends to achieve more highly than others, and the student who is less motivated than others tends to achieve less than others. Both of these relationships continue across time. This connection can be maintained even if total motivation is dropping for everyone (which is what is happening).

Cause and Effect?

One might ask the "chicken and egg" question about motivation and achievement. Which one causes the other? Perhaps higher-achieving students become more motivated to read and lower-achieving students lose their motivation. On the other side, the more motivated students may read, learn, and grow in achievement, whereas the less motivated ones avoid books and language in school. The best studies show that both of these are occurring. We have an intertwined connection. It may be called reciprocal determinism in technical circles. In studies of students in first grade through elementary and middle schools, motivation spurs achievement in reading and achievement spurs motivation. They are synergistic (Lepola, Salonen, & Vauras, 2000; Skinner & Belmont, 1993).

8

Struggling Readers

Boosting Motivation in Low Achievers

Sandra Jacobs Ivey and John T. Guthrie
University of Maryland

I n this chapter we focus on students who are the least motivated to read. This is a big group with a broad spectrum. Just as there are many ways to fail, there are many ways to be unmotivated. Because unmotivated students can be very different from each other, they require different approaches in the classroom. Just as there is more than one way to teach a concept for students who have different misunderstandings, there is more than one approach to motivating individuals who show different sources of motivational qualities. We identify three basic groups of students: (1) low achievers who are adequate readers, but are externally motivated; (2) low achievers who lack comprehension skills and are apathetic or resistant to reading; and (3) low achievers who lack word recognition and resist reading. We sketch alternative instruction in reading for these groups (Moore, Bean, Birdyshaw, & Rycik, 1999).

Our Challenges

Middle and high school students who read poorly have had very few positive experiences with books and texts. Naturally, they have developed deeply rooted negative beliefs. They exhibit low-efficacy toward reading and the reading process (Patterson & Elliott, 2006). These individuals have defeatist views—"I can't do this." They often cast blame on others for their perform-ance. They tend to believe that intelligence is inherited, and not gained by effort and persistence. Such readers lack motivation to read, as well as the metacognitive strategies necessary to improve their reading ability. As a result, these students devise coping mechanisms that not only protect them from appearing completely illiterate, but ironically, also strengthen their stance on the negative, downward trajectory. For example, many students adopt certain personas that will deflect their inability to read. Expending effort on diverting attention from the fact that they are experiencing prob-lems with reading, and not on strategies to improve reading, these students are actually perpetuating their history of low reading achievement.

This negative trajectory has additional characteristics. By the time strug-gling readers have reached high school, after frustration throughout their ele-mentary and middle school years, they are generally disengaged from the learning process. At best, they are apathetic or inattentive. Too often they exhibit poor academic concepts—even poor self-concepts—and usually attribute successes and failures to factors beyond their control. Many strug-gling readers demonstrate maladaptive social behaviors; they tend to be per-petually off-task, highly distractible, or exhibit poor behavior in class. In contrast, their behaviors can be on the opposite end of the spectrum, whereby the students exhibit a lack of energy—often napping in class—and make lit-tle or no effort in the academic process.

They can also be confrontational and angry. Acting out or disconnecting in class is an affective characteristic of disengagement that struggling readers often exhibit. Finally, truancy is another very common characteristic of this negative trajectory. Many of the students who do not drop out altogether attend irregularly, exert modest effort on schoolwork, and learn little (Finn, 2001).

National data show that student absenteeism (measured as cutting classes or skipping school for reasons other than illness) increases substantially with grade level—11% of eighth graders, 17% of tenth graders, and 33% of twelfth graders reported skipping at least one day of school during a four-week period (Stipek, 2004). These struggling readers' lack of success in reading places them at risk for the ultimate disengagement: dropping out of school (Finn, 2001).

Varieties of Unmotivated Readers

To show how unmotivated students differ from each other, we illustrate with 10th-grade high school students. At this grade level, about 20% of students in most schools achieve well and are internally motivated. They may be intrinsically motivated, may enjoy reading to learn, and may gain gratification from accruing knowledge. Even if not intrinsically motivated, they may identify themselves with reading. They may also hold strong beliefs that reading is important for their personal development and future benefit.

At Grade 10, however, some students are low in reading achievement primarily due to lack of internal motivation. Their reading achievement is more like that of a middle school student, which is two to three grade levels below expectation. As tenth graders reading at the seventh- to eighth-grade level, they are at a real disadvantage in all classes, although they may appear to get by.

These students are often externally motivated. They will work to avoid failing, but almost never for their own satisfaction. They seek a passing grade, or even a good grade; but they are at the external level (see Table 7.1 in Chapter 7). They have introjected (success seeking) and external (grade seeking) motivations. They may have decent grades in some courses, and may even have an adequate grade point average. But lacking the enjoyment and ownership of internal motivation, they only meet basic requirements. They do the minimal reading needed to look good. In the absence of internal motivation, they do not learn deeply in most subjects. Their reading appears flat. It does not increase or expand in sophistication. Because other more internally motivated students are advancing, the students with external-only motivations are stagnant. With every passing day, their futures, so dependent on schooling and literacy, are slipping away (Linnebrink & Pintrich, 2003).

Our first group, with solid external motivation, but little internal motivation, is moderately low in reading achievement. However, their cognitive equipment for learning from text is not obviously deficient. They can decode words adequately and are able to comprehend on-grade level text, if they give their commitment and effort. Unfortunately, their low internal motivation leads to deficiency of effort and perseverance. Both are necessary for long-term achievement in subject matters (Cappella & Weinstein, 2001).

The second group consists of resistant students who are lower in motivation. Rather than being externally motivated, they are demotivated. Beyond being indifferent, and not caring about school reading, they are resistant. Actively avoiding school reading, they may be brutally blunt, or clever, but the view is, "I hate to read, and I don't do it." From not reading, perhaps for several years, their knowledge base is impoverished. They have huge gaps in understanding about history, science, literature, or math (Stanovich, West, & Harrison, 1995). They often hold serious misconceptions about science topics, and their literary perceptions are very literal, at best.

The cognitive skills of reading comprehension in this group are low. They are not able to summarize a page of school text easily, even though they may read most of the words reasonably well. Although their oral reading fluency may be adequate, they are handicapped because they cannot pose useful questions, nor invoke other reading strategies to comprehend text (Klingner, Vaughn, Arguelles, Hughes, & Leftwich, 2004). Too often, they are not aware that they have not understood a passage, section, or chapter of a book. With few cognitive and metacognitive skills for reading comprehension, they are not proficient on a standardized reading achievement test. These students comprehend about the level of students in Grades 4 through 6.

A third group of low achievers in Grade 10 are at the lowest cognitive level. Generally at Grade 1 through 3 levels in word recognition and comprehension, these students are seriously disabled readers. Needless to say, they often resist reading, and they have learned avoidance strategies. Because they have struggled, suffered humiliation, and failed academically, they are likely to show a range of negative affects including denial of their problem, anger toward teachers, hostility toward school, anxiety about educational texts, and low self-concept for school reading.

Figure 8.1 shows the sizes of these three motivation problems in terms of the numbers of students who show these different characteristics. The largest group of low achievers in the Grade 10 population is about 50% of this age group. The students are externally motivated, and they show reading achievement at the middle school (Grades 7 to 8) level. The next group reads at the intermediate level (Grades 4 to 6) and is mostly resistant to reading, or possibly apathetic toward texts. The smallest group reads at the primary grade level (Grades 1 to 3). They are usually resistant to reading (Perie, Grigg, & Donahue, 2005).

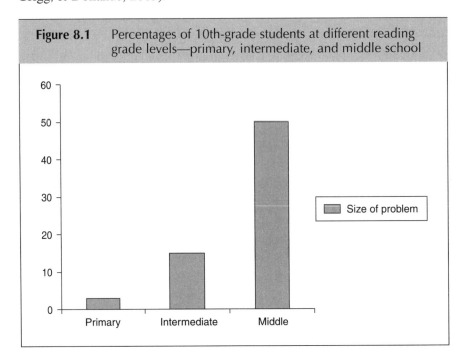

Figure 8.1   Percentages of 10th-grade students at different reading grade levels—primary, intermediate, and middle school

In Figure 8.2, we illustrate the types of reading issues for these three groups of struggling readers. It is evident that the high school students reading at the middle school level need motivational development to move their reading forward. Reading motivation is what determines their success or failure in reading. Their word recognition and comprehension skills are suitable for many reading tasks they face, but without development of more internal motivation, their achievement in reading and school is severely limited. For high school level students reading at the intermediate grade level, there is a strong need for cognitive strategies for reading comprehension. At the same time, these students are demotivated and require approaches to address their resistance. For high school students reading at the primary level, instruction in decoding, word recognition, and fluency are of paramount importance. These building blocks for comprehension and reading motivation must be addressed with intensive tutoring or small group teaching.

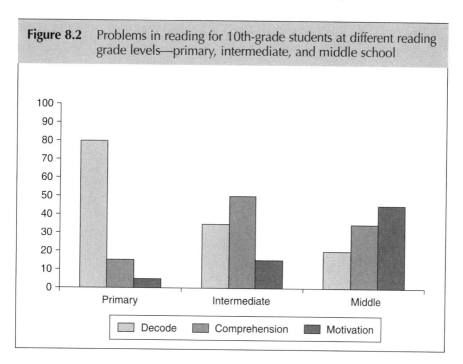

Figure 8.2   Problems in reading for 10th-grade students at different reading grade levels—primary, intermediate, and middle school

Externally Motivated Low Achievers

Many students claim that they simply do not have the time to read. Some are truly disinterested, while others are too busy. It seems that the unlimited access to cell phones, iPods, handheld game devices like PlayStation Portable (PSP) and Game Boy, cable or satellite television, and the Internet take adolescents' focus away from academic reading. Many diversions contend for adolescents' attention, time, and willingness to invest in their own literacy development.

The practice of reading seems to be dying out because of youth's preoccupation with playing computer and video games. Many adolescents even play their games online with opponents from all over the world. Like many other educators, we have wondered how to win the competition with video games and how to motivate students to value reading.

All may not totally be lost; some of the popular video games like Final Fantasy VII–IX have text that adolescents must read in order to progress in the game. We were able to observe these games. The text is narrative in nature and has sophisticated vocabulary on the high school level. When we interviewed a student about his reading habits, we asked about the amount of time he spent on activities in lieu of reading and about his opinion with regard to his peers' preferences to playing video games over reading. One student said, "It [playing video/computer games] is more engaging and visual; they are not choosing *not* to read, it's [reading] just something that does not come to mind." We then asked him, "Do you think that individuals who have difficulty in reading can play that sort of game?" He replied,

> That's the catch; the people who have trouble reading do not generally play that type of game. They play like sports games, like your football games. Final Fantasy is a role-playing game (RPG). It is essentially a story told through visuals. There's more to playing the game; you are following the story that unfolds just like a book, where you have a climax, you know, and things that lead up to the climax, and the end.

This student was honest when he confessed that he rarely reads, yet he is able to read the game's text and enjoy the narrative of the story—as he says, "the ending sequence." Interestingly enough, one's ability to function in our technological world will be divided along literacy lines. As educators, we need to consider the literacy identities learners construct in and out of school. By questioning our assumptions, we may come to the realization that adolescents' ways of thinking, knowing, believing, and acting shape the ways they connect with reading, writing, listening, and speaking (Moje, Dillon, & O'Brien, 2000).

The power of electronic media may contribute to a reduced level of reading for enjoyment among young adults. A national survey by the National Endowment for the Arts in 2004 showed the decline in reading literary materials (Hill, 2004). From 1982 to 2002, young adults in the 18 to 24 age range decreased in literary reading by 28%. In 2002, fewer than 42% said they had read a novel, short story, or play in the last 12 months. For adults in the 45 to 54 age group, there was a decline of only 6%, down to 52%. Although we do not know all the causes, literary reading for enjoyment (intrinsic motivation) is fast dropping, and is declining fastest among the youngest adults, those just out of school.

Approaches to Motivation for Moderately Struggling Readers

As we stated, moderately struggling readers tend to be externally motivated. Research indicates that externally motivated students often attempt to minimize their effort. Seventh graders who are grade oriented prefer superficial reading strategies, and they tend to avoid effortful cognitive strategies for text processing (Lau & Chan, 2003). Thus, low-achieving students who are externally motivated avoid deep thinking about text, which is needed for high achievement. At the same time, these externally motivated students do not consistently show intrinsic motivation for reading. To address the needs of these students, we provide support for intrinsic motivation through affording students choices and collaboration during reading. These students need a sense of ownership over what they read and how they read it. They need to take command of their books, whereas at present, their books have control over them. As we said in Chapter 3, giving choice is crucial. Choices of text are valuable. For struggling readers, this does not mean going to the library to find a book. It means giving choice about which passage to read first, which section to practice summarizing, which partner to take in discussing characters in a story, or which questions to answer for homework. Ownership grows in these small steps. If a student feels that this is *my* question, and I read *my* selection to answer it, and I have *my answer*, he owns that reading event. His connection to it means more than the grade, although he may like the grade, too. For his own question, he will read deeply, persevere, and gain an elaborated understanding (Boyd, 2002).

Teachers may suggest that if a student is struggling, he needs guidance. This is quite true. But guidance does not imply overcontrol, which is a major source of disengagement from reading. We give scaffolds to support choices. We start small and then increase amount of choice. In a history unit for Grade 10, a first choice we give to struggling readers may be to select which two-page segment to emphasize in a six-page section. The student decides which part to learn most thoroughly. Next, the student chooses a battle in which to specialize. While covering the total war, each student takes his battle. Later in the unit, each student reads and writes about his officer in the war. The scope of choice widens as students show that they are able to handle choices responsibly.

Scaffolding is the key to internal motivational development. Substantial experimental evidence suggests that providing autonomy support during instruction increases students' intrinsic motivation in reading to learn from content books (Reynolds & Symons, 2001), and learning among high school students (Reeve, Jang, Carrell, Jeon, & Barch, 2004).

For this group, we provide opportunities for productive social interaction in reading to learn. For secondary students especially, student collaboration in the form of accountable discussion about text content increases both motivation for reading and achievement in text comprehension (Applebee, Langer, Nystrand, & Gamoran, 2003). Collaboration is most valuable when it is *open*. This refers to the teacher posing broad questions that do not have factual answers. Students may also pose open questions. The discussion may occur between students, and it is supported by the teacher as a process. The teacher does not evaluate every statement for accuracy or acceptability. Students perceive this as intruding on their expression of opinion. While facts are vitally important, student perspective, argument, opinion, and input to a topic are central to their sense of involvement. Without involvement, motivation remains external, for the requirement, but not really for *me* as a person (Brozo & Hargis, 2003; Roe, 1997).

Collaboration may take many forms but is intended to give personal investment and return for reading the academic text. However, collaboration can be unproductive and a waste of time. The quality of time is based on teachers' scaffolding of the text (what we are talking about), the task (what questions or topics we are addressing), the time (how long we have for this work), and the significance (role of this discussion in the unit of study). Scaffolding includes the social side, too. We may set up partnerships, teams, or whole class interaction. The rules and roles of the interaction have to be set. Who talks? How long? Who listens, and for what purpose? How do we know we have had a good discussion? These are our judgments. The chapter on social interaction around text can be adapted, and it relates to struggling readers as well as other students (Wentzel, 1996).

Low Achievers Who Resist Reading

For all of us, students who resist reading are the most challenging. These students claim, "I don't read." Many of these students say they cannot read and fail to complete in-class reading, much less homework. They actively avoid reading and writing activities; as a result, their knowledge does not increase in a month—or a year—of school.

Students' resistance to reading is fed by two main sources. First, most of these students will claim that reading is boring. Although this claim sounds like an excuse for lack of effort, and may be an excuse for some students, boredom is a real problem. This is important because empirical studies show that adolescents report boredom in school to be associated with being forced to do meaningless tasks in reading and complete useless homework assignments (Assor, Kaplan, & Roth, 2002). Confirming this, Delespaul, Reis, and DeVries (2004) reported that boredom predicted resistance to study and escape behaviors among adolescents.

Boredom in reading comes from meaninglessness. If we cannot make sense of a formula, a diagram, or a book chapter, we find it boring. If something is totally devoid of meaning, we cannot connect to it, relate to it, or find it interesting. Students who are honestly bored by books usually do not bring any knowledge or relevant experience to the text. With no background, the text is very meaningless. For someone who knows nothing about astronomy, a serious astronomy book is boring. The same holds for Middle English poetry. If students cannot comprehend their books, they are repeatedly bored, and they soon resist the reading. So a student who frequently fails to comprehend text builds a resistance.

Another obvious source of resistance is low self-efficacy. If a student cannot make sense of a text after several attempts, he is likely to say, "I cannot read that book." He may jump to the conclusion that he cannot understand that subject. A student who does not grasp a poem written by Chaucer may quickly come to resist all poetry, even though he may be able to comprehend Emily Dickenson. When students fail repeatedly at a task, their perceived competence decreases, and elementary (Baker & Wigfield, 1999) and secondary students (Ryan, Patrick, & Shim, 2005) become resistant to reading as a result of these lowered competence beliefs. Students who fail early in their encounters with text often rebel from reading in that subject matter at that time. Their resistance will spread quickly with a few more frustrating experiences.

Approaches to Motivation for Resistant Students

We address resistant students by providing links between experience and text. For example, we show videos of curriculum-relevant content. Whether these are DVDs or Web-based videos, the visual images and narration are compelling. As well as being interesting, videos provide knowledge and multimedia experience on a topic. Such newfound knowledge about a subject matter can be connected to text, and thus, increase meaningfulness.

Students' resistance to text can also be reduced with hands-on experiences. For example, in science, observational activities and experiments are often fascinating and are rarely boring. When hands-on activities are connected to text consistently over time, reading growth increases (Guthrie, Wigfield, et al., 2006). This pattern also works for other types of real-world interactions such as enacting a scene from a play. Bringing a scene from a novel to life by writing a script for it and acting it out reduces resistance to text. Hands-on activities and enactments give students concrete experiences they can link to text; text is not boring, students can make meaning, and resistance is reduced.

For resistant students, we address low self-efficacy early and thoroughly. The biggest barrier to self-efficacy is difficult text. When students cannot easily read the main text aloud, they quickly conclude they cannot do the reading. Often they are right. Too frequently, books for required reading are two to four grade levels beyond the students' reading levels. (If a student cannot read a page aloud with fewer than five errors in word recognition, the text is too difficult.) Students react to the humiliation of trying to read such books by not reading. They resist the texts and the tasks that go with them. They disengage from literacy. Studies show that reading skills develop best when texts are matched to students' ability levels. Students gain in reading fluency and comprehension when the texts are decodable (e.g., they can read them aloud). Likewise, when struggling readers are compelled to read text on-grade level, their reading skills do not develop, according to a well-controlled experiment with disabled readers (O'Connor et al., 2002). In Chapter 5, which is on building self-efficacy, we emphasized using appropriate text in a thorough and systematic way. For struggling readers, this usually means that multiple texts are needed and that teachers must purchase new books. Trade books and Internet Web sites can be found that match students' levels in most subjects.

Needless to say, the text alone is not enough. Teachers who reach struggling readers give excellent feedback about progress with the appropriate texts. Helping students set realistic goals with appropriate text is an essential teacher action that we can master when the right text is available. For example, we support goal setting by saying, "Let's read three pages today because yesterday we read two pages." We then give feedback about progress toward success after the reading and a questioning or summary task is completed. Many teachers attempt to give students reading comprehension strategies such as questioning (Taboada & Guthrie, 2004) or thinking aloud during reading (Greenleaf, Schoenbach, Cziko, & Mueller, 2001). The potential for these strategies is high, but strategies are useful only if they are taught with readable text. If students cannot recognize the words in a passage, or cannot read it fluently, they cannot be taught a strategy by using that text. First, we find appropriately leveled text, and then we teach comprehension strategies and goal setting for self-efficacy.

A Learning Curriculum for Struggling Readers

Think about the needs of a struggling reader in Grade 10. This student may easily read at the Grades 5 to 8 levels, but let us say he reads at the Grade 7 level for this example. At this level, this student cannot read any of the science textbook, is not able to handle the volume of the novel in his English class, and can seldom form the connections to learn more than a few facts from history textbooks. In this scenario, the student is gaining no knowledge about science, English, or history. He is gaining almost no reading skill because he is doing such little reading. Even with a reading class, he is not likely to be reading for pleasure and cannot read course texts to productively use the skills he may learn in the reading lessons.

To catch up to his grade-level peers before high school graduation, this student will have to improve five grade levels in two years of school. Obviously, this is more than a 250% increase in rate of reading growth. Because this student requires help beyond simple decoding in comprehension, knowledge use, and cognitive reading strategies, this is utterly unrealistic. Unfortunately, this student will not learn to read at a sufficient level to gain knowledge from grade-level school texts. To confine this student to attempting to read three to five years beyond himself is to consign him to low knowledge growth. Furthermore, such confinement will reinforce the student's resistance that is certainly dampening his reading development. Without a new scenario, his potential for literacy in society is severely crippled.

The alternative for this student is to afford him books that are suitable for his knowledge development. He will learn science from a science text at the Grade 7 level, and will read a novel at the Grade 7 level. The teachers must be masterful in selecting texts, encouraging efficacy, reducing resistance, and focusing on his current knowledge. But with knowledge expansion as the goal and suitable text as a means, this student will gain knowledge. Such knowledge will enable him to meet some curriculum standards (at least ones he would not have met otherwise). It would enable him to use the reading skill he does possess, for Grade 7 reading comprehension is certainly far above zero. Of course, he should be taught reading strategies and possibly reading fluency in a reading course, if possible. Then, with leveled textbooks in content courses, his knowledge gains would enable him to access more complex textbooks in the future. By realigning the curriculum to be reading realistic and curriculum relevant, struggling readers can be ushered into the learning community.

Resistant Students Who Struggle to Recognize Words

Many educators struggle to prepare students with learning disabilities (LDs) to successfully achieve according to the rigor and pace of general education curricular demands. This presents a challenge because the majority of learning disabled students seem poorly prepared to succeed in high school (Deshler, Schumaker, & Lenz, 2001). Learning-disabled students exhibit the same characteristics as struggling or reluctant readers. Students with disabilities reach high school reading and writing, on average, at the fourth-grade level (Schumaker, Deshler, & McKnight, 2002). Many LD students have decoding and comprehension skills like those of students who are struggling in the general education classes. More specifically, LD students have poor memories, lack the prior knowledge that they need to understand the complex information being presented in their courses, and are concrete thinkers, who experience much difficulty distinguishing important from unimportant facts (Schumaker et al., 2002).

Overall, the characteristics that follow apply to LD students as well as struggling readers: poor attendance, high rates of course failures, poor self-concept, high rates of socially inappropriate behaviors, low grade-point averages, a history of academic underachievement, and high rates of dropouts in 11th and 12th grades. Students with LDs predictably pursue post secondary educations at a much lower rate than general education students—approximately 25% (Deshler et al., 2001).

Several trends in education exacerbate the negative trajectory that these students also face. These include curricular mandates, high-stakes testing, inclusion (Deshler et al., 2001), and programs for LD students that are outcome based within the context of mastering the general education's curriculum. The curricular mandates are problematic because LD students have much difficulty decoding expository texts whose readability is at or about the 10th-grade level and above. High-stakes testing is especially problematic for this population for three basic reasons: (1) LD students generally do not know basic math facts; (2) the majority of LD students have difficulty with writing complete sentences, so longer, more organized writing (e.g., essays) is highly improbable; and (3) most LD students do not know how to study for tests, especially if the tests require large amounts of information to be processed. As a result, a large percentage of LD students fail state assessments. In 1997, 21% of students with disabilities did not meet graduation requirements by failing the state exam in Indiana.

Instructional Approaches for Resistant Students With Word Reading Deficits

For these students, beginning reading must be taught. Word-level skill instruction using scientifically based research is highly effective for increasing word recognition accuracy and speed (Torgesen, 2004). At the elementary and middle school levels, a large proportion of readers who are struggling at the word level can be taught effectively, using low teacher-pupil ratios and explicit instruction.

The Strategic Instruction Model (SIM) developed by Schumaker and Deshler (1988) is an instructional program designed to help students with learning disabilities succeed in their general education classes. SIM implements the use of curricular materials that appeal to different learning styles, strategies for students to gain comprehension, and routines for teachers to meet the needs of this population of diverse learners. The learning strategies in SIM include (1) reading, whereby paraphrasing, self-questioning, visual imagery, and word identification skills are taught; (2) storing and remembering information; (3) expressing information; (4) demonstrating competence; (5) social interaction; and (6) mathematics. All are areas where LD students have the greatest difficulties.

The Word Identification Strategy developed by Lenz and Hughes (1990) helps struggling readers and LD students to decode and identify unfamiliar words, and focuses on the foundations of most polysyllabic words in English. Students are instructed to identify and pronounce word components such as prefixes, suffixes, and stems, and then apply three rules for syllabication to the stem word. There are seven steps in the identification process: (1) discover the context, (2) isolate the prefix, (3) separate the suffix, (4) say the stem, (5) examine the stem, (6) get help and check with someone, and (7) use a dictionary. On first look, this strategy seems time consuming, but Lenz and Hughes (1990) suggested that all steps be followed, but only for the most critical, unfamiliar words, or for the words most critical to understanding the text. After listening to our at-risk high school students read aloud, we are willing to use this strategy.

One of the most promising instructional interventions to promote adolescents' literacy development is peer-assisted learning strategies (PALS). This construct pairs higher- and lower-performing students in general education classrooms to work on structured reading activities: sustained reading by each partner, followed by the higher-performing student asking the lower-performing student who, what, where, when, and why questions

(L. S. Fuchs, D. Fuchs, & Kazdan, 1999). PALS was primarily designed for elementary-age students, but has long since been thought to be an effective strategy for secondary-level students. Classwide peer tutoring has been observed to dramatically increase long-term reading achievement with low- and average-achieving students, as well as students with learning disabilities. Classwide peer tutoring has spread, and hybrid versions of the methods have been developed and tested, extending to include summarization and prediction (Fuchs et al., 1999).

Teachers form PALS pairs throughout their entire classroom. In the reading practice, the higher-performing student will read first as a model for the lower-performing student. The reading material selected is appropriate for the lower reader's ability. Both read the same material. Every day of PALS activity, each student in the pair reads aloud for five minutes of sustained reading. Interestingly enough, reading pairs are assigned to one of two teams for which they will earn points for correctly completing reading activities and for appropriately demonstrating tutoring behavior. Upon closer look, PALS practice is a reward system whereby each pair keeps track of points on a consecutively numbered score card, which represents joint effort and achievement, and at the end of the week, scores are totaled for the teams. The winning team is applauded by fellow classmates. Every four weeks, new reading pairs are formed, the motivational system combining competitive (team vs. team) and cooperative (combined effort of the pair) structures (Fuchs et al., 1999).

While reading comprehension and fluency are being improved, the most potent aspect of the peer-assisted approach lies in the fact that it positively affects students' self-efficacy toward reading. Fuchs et al's. (1999) study suggested that students developed more positive beliefs about working hard to improve their reading. Indeed, students are motivated when they express interest in an academic task, feel excited about it, and think that it is important and worthwhile. Motivation research has shown that these beliefs and feelings about interest and value lead to increased student engagement and learning (Linnenbrink & Pintrich, 2003). If students are motivated to read in the peer-assisted approach, then it is likely that they will spend more time reading, thus becoming better readers.

Secondary struggling readers have longer histories of failure that further complicate efforts at remediation. PALS has not been studied as extensively in the high school setting. The basic high school schedule offers a logistical problem with implementation of the program. Another problem is not having the appropriate resources available, thus providing no natural curricular opportunity for reading instruction to occur. The reinforcement system must be structured and tangible for struggling readers at the secondary level.

Perhaps a modification to the approach will include engaging the students in a discussion about appropriate or suitable rewards. Giving students an opportunity to choose their rewards can help motivate them to carry out the practice. Although a healthy dose of competition can be motivating, we have concerns about whether PALS encourages students to set mastery goals. Sustained reading for five minutes seems too short a time for high school students. Furthermore, student pairs should be rotated more often than the four-week standard. All in all, there needs to be access to high-interest, age-appropriate, and reading-level-appropriate reading materials, longer reading sessions, and greater incentives to read.

9

Next Steps for Teachers

John T. Guthrie
University of Maryland

Y ou may have read this entire book, or you may have skimmed it. Perhaps you took a shortcut to the ending statement. Whatever your circumstance, you are asking, "What shall we do to promote motivation and engagement in reading?"

Most teachers do not have to be persuaded that students need more motivation. Except for the few teachers with energized, devoted students, motivation is a challenge at some level. Motivational problems are a classroom reality, and that reality is getting starker every year and even daily. So why did we offer an entire first chapter on the *challenge*? The reason for Chapter 1 is that we wanted to underscore the wide scope of motivation. We aimed to document the depth of this dilemma for educators. In this chapter, we offer a blueprint for change. It outlines a plan for teacher action.

Identifying One Motivation to Address

Step 1 is to start small. While it seems amorphous, motivation can be tackled in parts. The strategy we suggest is *divide and conquer*. Begin by thinking of one type of motivation in your students, classes, and school that you want to address. You may select the most severe motivational issue, or you may identify a very approachable motivational problem that you believe you can successfully treat without overhauling your entire educational philosophy.

Although motivation is sort of one thing, motivation is also many-splendored. It is multifaceted, and its many sides are slightly different. These various aspects of motivation are distinct enough that they respond to alternative teaching approaches. You do not do quite the same thing for students who need ownership as you do for students who need a stronger self-efficacy. Yet, motivation is one thing because these different aspects are linked together. Ultimately, they are mutually supportive. Engaging teaching will integrate support for all of these motivational dimensions.

For review, the motivations that we portrayed in this book were the following: (1) *mastery goals*, which are students' purposes of reading for understanding, rather than reading for a test score or a display of performance; (2) *control and choice*, which relate to students' ownership over their reading; (3) *social interaction* in reading, which generates enthusiasm for the text and its contents; (4) *self-efficacy*, which is confidence in one's ability to read and comprehend well; and (5) *interest*, which is the feeling that a text or topic is appealing or fascinating.

Our suggestion is to identify one of these motivations as your priority. Do you think your students primarily lack mastery goals, ownership, self-efficacy, or some other motivation in reading? Obviously, students at different achievement levels will have different motivational needs. We discussed those diverse needs in Chapter 8. All except the most intrinsically motivated readers, however, can benefit from instructional support for their motivational development.

You may identify a motivational starting point by talking about and debating this issue with your colleagues. Perhaps you form a team at your grade level and subject matter in your school. Perhaps you enter a district-wide study group. Your group can discuss this at your own direction, or you could use resources in this book. For example, you could take the questionnaires for teachers and use them as discussion starting points. We make suggestions for how to do this in the sections of this chapter on short-term planning and long-term planning. You could administer the student questionnaire, code it to the standards, and discuss it, as outlined in another section of this chapter. You may entertain other research or recruit experts to assist you in finding a good beginning. You may also decide to address all these motivations and work toward increasing all the associated practices for engagement support.

Selecting Several Instructional Practices to Initiate Motivation

As each chapter shows, there are many ways to support motivation. You are already doing some of them or else you would not be surviving as a teacher. Nevertheless, you can do more—perhaps much more—for students' motivational development. Each chapter offers five to seven teaching approaches or techniques that can fuel the motivation addressed in that chapter.

As the chapters indicate, some instructional practices will encourage more than one of the motivations we describe. You can nourish some motivations by more than one aspect of your teaching approach and classroom context. We organized the students' motivations and instructional approaches in this way to give you a handle. Although we believe in the priorities for motivations and teaching practices we propose, we realize there is a web of possibilities.

In brief, the students' motivations and teachers' instructional practices portrayed in this book are outlined next.

1. *Mastery goals*, which are students' purposes of reading for understanding, rather than reading for a test score or a reward:
   a. providing mastery goals
   b. making tasks relevant
   c. using hands-on activities
   d. transforming text to meaning
   e. scaffolding mastery motivation
   f. providing reteach opportunities
   g. rewarding effort over performance

2. *Control and choice*, which relate to students' ownership over their reading:
   a. ownership of text
   b. options for how to learn
   c. input into curriculum
   d. self-selection of knowledge displays
   e. voice in standards for evaluating
   f. inquiry projects

3. *Social interaction* in reading, which generates enthusiasm for reading:
   a. open discussions
   b. student-led discussion groups
   c. collaborative reasoning
   d. teachers relating to individuals

   e. partnerships for reading
   f. socially constructing the management
   g. scaffolding social motivations over time

4. *Self-efficacy*, which is confidence in one's ability to read well:
   a. recognizing the gap between my students and their texts
   b. locating texts matched to students
   c. establishing initial confidence
   d. building confidence through goal setting
   e. assuring enabling skills for comprehending the text

5. *Interest*, which is the feeling that a text or topic is appealing or fascinating:
   a. making real-world connections
   b. personalizing with questioning
   c. extending intrinsic interests
   d. self-expressing
   e. puzzling

Planning Short-Term Change

If you are following our game plan, you have identified one key motivation from our set of interrelated ones. You have also selected at least four instructional practices that will foster that motivation. We say at least four because one lonely practice will not have a high impact, although it may occasionally be valuable. We suggest four even though we recommend five to seven practices, because there is not one magic bullet. No single set is miraculously better than others. This parallels the teaching of reading strategies. Many approaches to improving students' questioning, concept mapping, inferencing, and summarizing are valuable.

For motivation, the instructional practices presented here meet twin standards. First, they are research-based because studies in the scientific tradition show they are superior to other instructional conditions and comparisons. In each chapter, we submitted a sample of experimental and other scientific literature related to classroom motivation. Second, these practices are tried and true. Successfully implemented by at least one teacher in one subject matter, they are legitimated by successful classroom trials.

To begin short-term planning, take stock of your current teaching. For each instructional practice, ask yourself the following seven questions:

1. Do I do this already?
2. How often do I do this?

3. When do I do this?
4. How well does it work?
5. How can I do this more?
6. How can I do this better?
7. How can I connect this to my current teaching more deeply?

These questions assume that you are familiar with these practices. They are not revolutionary, for the most part. You are most likely already implementing some of them to some degree. Your goal is expanding, permeating, deepening, accelerating, and formalizing this practice to make it a centerpiece of your teaching. When you accomplish this, you will transform your students' reading experience.

For short-term planning, you want to ask, "How can I do this tomorrow?" If you intend to increase students' motivation through control and choice, your self-question is, "What choice can I give my students tomorrow?" As shown in Chapter 3, this may be a choice of text (what to read), strategy (how to learn from the text), task (how to show learning from the text), social interaction (how to discuss the text), or evaluation (how to assess or display knowledge gained from text). Expanding this slightly to, "What choice am I going to give tomorrow that I did not give yesterday?" initiates the bridge toward an autonomy supportive and motivating classroom.

The time span of short-term change is about 20 days; plan for providing choices for about four school weeks. In less time than that, you may not have found the right motivating choices. If you give too many choices, and students are lost or unproductive, you want to scale back. Soon, you will figure out the optimal choices for your students and for your subject matter, in keeping with your personal style.

Recall also that the goal of supporting students' motivation is to increase the amount of time they devote to deep reading. Choice is the means, not the end, of motivational support. The goal is motivated, meaningful reading, not merely a series of fun choices. You do not need more than 20 days to see the benefit or to diagnose your own implementation of this instructional practice.

Planning Long-Term Change

Long-term change is more like a school year. You may want to work alone, but it is easier to work along. To tackle this ambitious agenda, form a grade-level team, or join a school group or district task force. Rethink your instruction and your curriculum more broadly. For this, you can raise the same questions as for short-term planning. For an entire course, or a course sequence, ask these seven questions:

1. Does the course do this already?
2. How often does the course do this?
3. When does the course do this?
4. How well does it work?
5. How can we do this more frequently?
6. How can we do this better?
7. How can the course connect to this practice more deeply?

You may want to use tools offered in this book in this endeavor. You could do any of the following: take the teacher questionnaire and use it for a study-group discussion; administer the student questionnaire and discuss your findings in your team; or apply the teacher questionnaire to the curriculum by following the suggestions at the end of this chapter.

Phasing in Support for All Motivations and Implementing All Practices

Thus far, we have described one motivation and a few instructional practices. This is a crucial starting point. But what is the ending point? Our aim consists of full-scale, systemic, motivational support across the subject matters in a school. The mature school has all of the motivational practices continually occurring in all of the subject matters. Student reading engagement is an aim of the teachers and a mission of the school. Engagement in reading is integral to the design of the curriculum. Appraisal of student engagement is regular, and widespread engaged reading is celebrated. Phasing in such systemic support for motivation and engagement promises to bring multiple benefits to the diverse constituencies of a school.

Engagement in reading cannot be the sole goal. Test scores, recognized achievement, and student qualifications for further education are crucial. We need to embrace achievement. What we seek is to make engagement a pathway to achievement. A study of fifteen-year-olds in 30 countries showed that reading engagement correlated with reading achievement in every country including the United States, European nations, Asian countries, and others (Kirsch et al., 2002). Engagement in reading, then, is a powerful tool. It is a long lever for school success. Not only is reading engagement enriching for students, it is rewarding for teachers. Beyond being a model for students' participation in the classroom, reading engagement is a vehicle for school improvement. Following this chapter you'll find the questionnaires and resources that provide the rubrics, coding schemes, and standards for use in taking the steps we have discussed.

Tools for Teachers

Student Questionnaire. Administer the questionnaire in your classroom. Read the directions aloud. Then, read the questions aloud with the students if it is feasible or necessary. Advanced students can read them for themselves. Code all the items with a 1–4 as follows: Very true = 4; Somewhat true = 3; Not very true = 2; and Not at all true = 1. There are five exceptions, which are items 4, 8, 12, 16, and 20. These items are coded in reverse: Very true = 1; Somewhat true = 2; Not very true = 3; and Not at all true = 4. For each student, add the scores for each item. The total score from 20 to 80 is the student's level of engagement.

Standards of performance are as follows:

71–80 Engaged
56–70 Emergent
41–55 Apathetic
20–40 Disengaged

Students at the engaged level are reasonably involved and enthusiastic about the context for reading engagement in your classroom. If their responses are fully candid, they see strong support for their reading engagement in your classroom.

Students at the emergent level are on the borderline. In their eyes, the classroom is not fully or consistently supporting their engaged reading. They could become more engaged in reading with your support through planning and attention to the recommended practices.

Students at the apathetic level believe they are not receiving a high amount of support for motivation to read. While the classroom context occasionally nurtures their reading, these students experience many gaps in support. As a result, they may not be reading deeply or succeeding to their potential. There are likely to be practices that you can use to increase the reading engagement of these students.

Students at the disengaged level may be in a real crisis. Their perception is that they are not well supported to engage in reading. Consequently, they could be neglecting reading and not learning much from text. Very substantial rethinking of the classroom goals, materials, organization, and the curriculum may be required. Students at this level are indicating that educators are advised to think outside the box to increase reading motivation and engagement.

Teacher Questionnaire. For the teacher questionnaire, there are several parallels. Administer it to yourself or take it with your team. Read the directions and proceed. When you finish, code all the items with a 1–4 as follows: Strongly agree = 4; Agree = 3; Disagree = 2; Strongly disagree = 1. There are five exceptions, which are items 4, 8, 12, 16, and 20. These items are coded in reverse: Strongly agree = 1; Agree = 2; Disagree = 3; Strongly disagree = 4. Add the scores for each item. The total score from 20 to 80 is your level of support for reading engagement.

Standards of performance are as follows:

71–80 Affirming Engagement
56–70 Fairly Supportive
41–55 Needs Attention
20–40 Needs Improvement

If you scored at the Affirming Engagement level, you are supporting engaged reading. We offer commendations on your teaching. Perhaps you can mentor other teachers.

If you scored at the Fairly Supportive level, you are very aware of these issues. You are likely to have exciting events in your classroom, but students need more support for their reading motivation. You might attempt to extend your thinking along the lines suggested in this book.

If you scored at the Needs Attention level, support for reading engagement is an issue that is calling for your thinking. You may not have paid attention to how the curriculum supports reading engagement. It is possible that you have had other priorities. You and your students, however, will likely be rewarded by your increasing support for reading engagement. You may have some compliant students or some troublesome ones. Students may or may not be engaged readers, but you could make some revisions in your strategies to foster their reading engagement.

If you scored at the Needs Improvement level, you may want to address your classroom practices related to support for engagement in reading. It is likely that many of your students will benefit from rethinking some of your assumptions and approaches. In some cases, students may be responsible for their own disengagement. If you move thoughtfully toward some of the recommended practices, however, your students in this course will likely show more motivation and commitment to reading.

Curriculum Rubric. We invite you to appraise your curriculum and instruction using the Curriculum Evaluation Rubric for Reading Engagement found in Resource E. We supply the rubric and guidance for applying it in the Resource section. This instrument is based on the scientific research literature on processes of students' motivation and the classroom influences on engagement. Use the descriptions of practices in the book to complete the evaluation rubric. The outcome will show the extent to which the curriculum explicitly supports student motivations of mastery goals, autonomy, social interaction, self-efficacy, and interest in reading.

Questionnaires

Student Questionnaire for Meaning Is Motivating

Name _____ **Date** _____

Directions to Student

Please answer the items below. It is important to be honest. Make your own decisions. There are no right or wrong answers. This information will NOT be used for any grade and it will not be sent to your parents or caregivers.

Circle one response for each item under the sentence.

Example:

A. My name is important to me.

$\quad$ (Strongly Agree) $\qquad$ Agree $\qquad$ Disagree $\qquad$ Strongly Disagree

$\quad$ If you strongly agree that your name is important to you, circle Strongly Agree, as above.

---

1. In this class, the teacher expects me to explain the ideas.

   Strongly Agree $\qquad$ Agree $\qquad$ Disagree $\qquad$ Strongly Disagree

2. In this class, we have to remember a lot of information we do not use.

   Strongly Agree $\qquad$ Agree $\qquad$ Disagree $\qquad$ Strongly Disagree

3. The teacher in this class wants us to understand the material we read.

   Strongly Agree $\qquad$ Agree $\qquad$ Disagree $\qquad$ Strongly Disagree

4. This teacher is mostly concerned with how we perform on tests.

   Strongly Agree $\qquad$ Agree $\qquad$ Disagree $\qquad$ Strongly Disagree

5. The topics in this class all fit together so I can understand them.

   Strongly Agree $\qquad$ Agree $\qquad$ Disagree $\qquad$ Strongly Disagree

6. My teacher gives me many ways to show my knowledge of this subject.

   Strongly Agree $\qquad$ Agree $\qquad$ Disagree $\qquad$ Strongly Disagree

7. We only have one chance to learn the important material in this class.

   Strongly Agree $\qquad$ Agree $\qquad$ Disagree $\qquad$ Strongly Disagree

8. This teacher helps us understand the main points and the examples for them.

   Strongly Agree $\qquad$ Agree $\qquad$ Disagree $\qquad$ Strongly Disagree

Thank you.

Teacher Questionnaire for Meaning Is Motivating

Name _____ **Date** _____

Directions to Teacher

Please answer the items below. It is important to be honest. Make your own decisions about each item. There are no right or wrong answers. This information will NOT be provided to others, unless you approve.

Circle one response for each item under the sentence.

Example:

A. My teaching is important to me.

(Strongly Agree)   Agree   Disagree   Strongly Disagree

If you strongly agree that your teaching is important to you, circle Strongly Agree, as above.

---

1. My lectures have all the information students need for tests.

   Strongly Agree   Agree   Disagree   Strongly Disagree

2. I help students tackle the challenging content in the texts in this class.

   Strongly Agree   Agree   Disagree   Strongly Disagree

3. I always post content goals and objectives for reading.

   Strongly Agree   Agree   Disagree   Strongly Disagree

4. I give grades based totally on students' test scores.

   Strongly Agree   Agree   Disagree   Strongly Disagree

5. I expect students to give reasons for all their answers or ideas.

   Strongly Agree   Agree   Disagree   Strongly Disagree

6. My assignments require students to show what they learned from text in their own way.

   Strongly Agree   Agree   Disagree   Strongly Disagree

7. Student viewpoints about the readings are just as important as the text itself.

   Strongly Agree   Agree   Disagree   Strongly Disagree

8. A priority in this class is recalling a lot of information accurately.

   Strongly Agree   Agree   Disagree   Strongly Disagree

Thank you.

Student Questionnaire for Control and Choice

Name _____ **Date** _____

Directions to Student

Please answer the items below. It is important to be honest. Make your own decisions. There are no right or wrong answers. This information will NOT be used for any grade and it will not be sent to your parents or caregivers.

Circle one response for each item under the sentence.

Example:

A. My name is important to me.

(Strongly Agree)   Agree   Disagree   Strongly Disagree

If you strongly agree that your name is important to you, circle Strongly Agree, as above.

---

1. My teacher allows me to choose books I want to read at least once a month.

   Strongly Agree   Agree   Disagree   Strongly Disagree

2. I do not have a chance to decide anything in this class.

   Strongly Agree   Agree   Disagree   Strongly Disagree

3. My teacher allows me to help decide which types of assignments to do.

   Strongly Agree   Agree   Disagree   Strongly Disagree

4. The readings are set for me in this class.

   Strongly Agree   Agree   Disagree   Strongly Disagree

5. I have choices about what to read or study in this class.

   Strongly Agree   Agree   Disagree   Strongly Disagree

6. I feel motivated to read at home for this class.

   Strongly Agree   Agree   Disagree   Strongly Disagree

7. This teacher tells us what to do.

   Strongly Agree   Agree   Disagree   Strongly Disagree

8. My teacher asks for students' opinions and viewpoints.

   Strongly Agree   Agree   Disagree   Strongly Disagree

Thank you.

Teacher Questionnaire for Control and Choice

Name _____ **Date** _____

Directions to Teacher

Please answer the items below. It is important to be honest. Make your own decisions about each item. There are no right or wrong answers. This information will NOT be provided to others, unless you approve.

Circle one response for each item under the sentence.

Example:

A. My teaching is important to me.

(Strongly Agree)   Agree   Disagree   Strongly Disagree

If you strongly agree that your teaching is important to you, circle Strongly Agree, as above.

---

1. This class follows the textbook and the curriculum guide precisely.

   Strongly Agree   Agree   Disagree   Strongly Disagree

2. I allow students to select topics for study in this course.

   Strongly Agree   Agree   Disagree   Strongly Disagree

3. I ask for student input about projects and activities in this class.

   Strongly Agree   Agree   Disagree   Strongly Disagree

4. I choose the textbook and everything we read.

   Strongly Agree   Agree   Disagree   Strongly Disagree

5. I request student opinions about the content daily.

   Strongly Agree   Agree   Disagree   Strongly Disagree

6. Students direct their own reading much of the time.

   Strongly Agree   Agree   Disagree   Strongly Disagree

7. I teach students to take initiative in their reading.

   Strongly Agree   Agree   Disagree   Strongly Disagree

8. Students in this class are not able to make sensible choices about the course.

   Strongly Agree   Agree   Disagree   Strongly Disagree

Thank you.

Student Questionnaire for Reading Is Social

Name _____ **Date** _____

Directions to Student

Please answer the items below. It is important to be honest. Make your own decisions. There are no right or wrong answers. This information will NOT be used for any grade and it will not be sent to your parents or caregivers.

Circle one response for each item under the sentence.

Example:

A. My name is important to me.

(Strongly Agree)   Agree   Disagree   Strongly Disagree

  If you strongly agree that your name is important to you, circle Strongly Agree, as above.

---

1. When I am with my classmates, I feel accepted.

   Strongly Agree   Agree   Disagree   Strongly Disagree

2. When working in groups, I often feel left out.

   Strongly Agree   Agree   Disagree   Strongly Disagree

3. I learn best during group reading and writing activities.

   Strongly Agree   Agree   Disagree   Strongly Disagree

4. I usually do not try to help my classmates with their problems in reading.

   Strongly Agree   Agree   Disagree   Strongly Disagree

5. I sometimes talk to the teacher about books I read.

   Strongly Agree   Agree   Disagree   Strongly Disagree

6. When the teacher asks, I make suggestions about how this class is run.

   Strongly Agree   Agree   Disagree   Strongly Disagree

7. When discussing what we read, I do not get along with other students.

   Strongly Agree   Agree   Disagree   Strongly Disagree

8. When I am with my teacher, I feel important.

   Strongly Agree   Agree   Disagree   Strongly Disagree

Thank you.

Teacher Questionnaire for Reading Is Social

Name _____ **Date** _____

Directions to Teacher

Please answer the items below. It is important to be honest. Make your own decisions about each item. There are no right or wrong answers. This information will NOT be provided to others, unless you approve.

Circle one response for each item under the sentence.

Example:

A. My teaching is important to me.

(Strongly Agree)   Agree   Disagree   Strongly Disagree

If you strongly agree that your teaching is important to you, circle Strongly Agree, as above.

---

1. There is too little time to get to know students well.

   Strongly Agree   Agree   Disagree   Strongly Disagree

2. I provide students with social interactions that promote their reading.

   Strongly Agree   Agree   Disagree   Strongly Disagree

3. I ask for student suggestions about how to organize this class.

   Strongly Agree   Agree   Disagree   Strongly Disagree

4. I have to punish many students in this class to get them to follow the rules.

   Strongly Agree   Agree   Disagree   Strongly Disagree

5. I allow students the opportunity to form their own collaborative groups.

   Strongly Agree   Agree   Disagree   Strongly Disagree

6. I monitor to make sure all students participate when I ask them to work together.

   Strongly Agree   Agree   Disagree   Strongly Disagree

7. I encourage students to discuss the reading with each other.

   Strongly Agree   Agree   Disagree   Strongly Disagree

8. I believe students learn most when they work on their own.

   Strongly Agree   Agree   Disagree   Strongly Disagree

Thank you.

Student Questionnaire for Self-Efficacy

Name _____ Date _____

Directions to Student

Please answer the items below. It is important to be honest. Make your own decisions. There are no right or wrong answers. This information will NOT be used for any grade and it will not be sent to your parents or caregivers.

Circle one response for each item under the sentence.

Example:

A. My name is important to me.

(Strongly Agree)   Agree   Disagree   Strongly Disagree

If you strongly agree that your name is important to you, circle Strongly Agree, as above.

---

1. I can comprehend the textbook used in this class.

   Strongly Agree   Agree   Disagree   Strongly Disagree

2. In this class, I cannot read the textbook out loud without making mistakes.

   Strongly Agree   Agree   Disagree   Strongly Disagree

3. I can always relate what I read in this class to the main topic we are studying.

   Strongly Agree   Agree   Disagree   Strongly Disagree

4. I have a difficult time reading the textbook in this class because there are too many new vocabulary words.

   Strongly Agree   Agree   Disagree   Strongly Disagree

5. I set specific goals for my reading in this class.

   Strongly Agree   Agree   Disagree   Strongly Disagree

6. I can complete the reading assignments given in this class.

   Strongly Agree   Agree   Disagree   Strongly Disagree

7. In this class, I just skim the book to answer the questions quickly.

   Strongly Agree   Agree   Disagree   Strongly Disagree

8. My teacher helps me understand how to read the textbook in this class.

   Strongly Agree   Agree   Disagree   Strongly Disagree

Thank you.

Teacher Questionnaire for Self-Efficacy

Name _____ **Date** _____

Directions to Teacher

Please answer the items below. It is important to be honest. Make your own decisions about each item. There are no right or wrong answers. This information will NOT be provided to others, unless you approve.

Circle one response for each item under the sentence.

Example:

A. My teaching is important to me.

　(Strongly Agree)　　Agree　　Disagree　　Strongly Disagree

　If you strongly agree that your teaching is important to you, circle Strongly Agree, as above.

---

1. In this class, the texts do not always align with my content goals.

   Strongly Agree　　Agree　　Disagree　　Strongly Disagree

2. I must help my students relate their prior knowledge to new information in the textbook.

   Strongly Agree　　Agree　　Disagree　　Strongly Disagree

3. I make certain the students can read the text out loud easily.

   Strongly Agree　　Agree　　Disagree　　Strongly Disagree

4. I do not have time to help students set their own goals for reading.

   Strongly Agree　　Agree　　Disagree　　Strongly Disagree

5. I help students gain confidence in reading the texts for this course.

   Strongly Agree　　Agree　　Disagree　　Strongly Disagree

6. I can predict what texts students will misunderstand.

   Strongly Agree　　Agree　　Disagree　　Strongly Disagree

7. My students are completely capable of reading the homework assignments.

   Strongly Agree　　Agree　　Disagree　　Strongly Disagree

8. On assessments, my students show they have misunderstood important parts of the text.

   Strongly Agree　　Agree　　Disagree　　Strongly Disagree

Thank you.

Student Questionnaire for Interest in Reading

Name _____ **Date** _____

Directions to Student

Please answer the items below. It is important to be honest. Make your own decisions. There are no right or wrong answers. This information will NOT be used for any grade and it will not be sent to your parents or caregivers.

Circle one response for each item under the sentence.

Example:

A. My name is important to me.

(Strongly Agree)   Agree   Disagree   Strongly Disagree

If you strongly agree that your name is important to you, circle Strongly Agree, as above.

---

1. The teacher relates the reading to my interests.

   Strongly Agree   Agree   Disagree   Strongly Disagree

2. The reading material in this class does not connect to the outside world.

   Strongly Agree   Agree   Disagree   Strongly Disagree

3. We do projects about what we read in this class.

   Strongly Agree   Agree   Disagree   Strongly Disagree

4. I usually cannot relate to what I read in this class.

   Strongly Agree   Agree   Disagree   Strongly Disagree

5. I say what I think about the books in this course.

   Strongly Agree   Agree   Disagree   Strongly Disagree

6. In this class, I can connect the reading to my experiences.

   Strongly Agree   Agree   Disagree   Strongly Disagree

7. My grades are completely based on the teacher's quizzes and tests.

   Strongly Agree   Agree   Disagree   Strongly Disagree

8. My teacher encourages us to ask a lot of questions about what we read.

   Strongly Agree   Agree   Disagree   Strongly Disagree

Thank you.

Teacher Questionnaire for Interest in Reading

Name _____ **Date** _____

Directions to Teacher

Please answer the items below. It is important to be honest. Make your own decisions about each item. There are no right or wrong answers. This information will NOT be provided to others, unless you approve.

Circle one response for each item under the sentence.

Example:

   A. My teaching is important to me.

   (Strongly Agree)   Agree   Disagree   Strongly Disagree

   If you strongly agree that your teaching is important to you, circle
   Strongly Agree, as above.

---

1. I think the subject matter in the text is the most important part of the course.

   Strongly Agree   Agree   Disagree   Strongly Disagree

2. I give students hands-on experiences related to the texts.

   Strongly Agree   Agree   Disagree   Strongly Disagree

3. I ask students for their opinions about the text content.

   Strongly Agree   Agree   Disagree   Strongly Disagree

4. We have time to discuss applications of what we read about to other situations.

   Strongly Agree   Agree   Disagree   Strongly Disagree

5. I use the students' questions as goals for reading.

   Strongly Agree   Agree   Disagree   Strongly Disagree

6. I link the topics of this course to students' experiences very frequently.

   Strongly Agree   Agree   Disagree   Strongly Disagree

7. Usually I help students relate the reading to their interests.

   Strongly Agree   Agree   Disagree   Strongly Disagree

8. Tests and quizzes determine the students' grades almost totally.

   Strongly Agree   Agree   Disagree   Strongly Disagree

Thank you.

Student Questionnaire for Reading in School

Name _____ **Date** _____

Directions to Student

Please answer the items below. It is important to be honest. Make your own decisions. There are no right or wrong answers. This information will NOT be used for any grade and it will not be sent to your parents or caregivers.

Circle one response for each item under the sentence.

Example:

A. My name is important to me.

(Very true)   Somewhat true   Not very true   Not at all true

If it is true that your name is important to you, circle Very true, as above.

---

1. In this class the teacher expects me to explain the ideas.

   Very true   Somewhat true   Not very true   Not at all true

2. The teacher encourages me to take risks as long as I am learning.

   Very true   Somewhat true   Not very true   Not at all true

3. I see how each reading ties to what we already learned in the class.

   Very true   Somewhat true   Not very true   Not at all true

4. This teacher is mainly concerned with how we perform on tests.

   Very true   Somewhat true   Not very true   Not at all true

5. My teacher allows me to choose books I want to read at least once a month.

   Very true   Somewhat true   Not very true   Not at all true

6. My teacher allows me to help decide which assignments to do.

   Very true   Somewhat true   Not very true   Not at all true

7. My teacher asks for students' opinions and viewpoints.

   Very true   Somewhat true   Not very true   Not at all true

8. This teacher tells us what to do all the time.

   Very true   Somewhat true   Not very true   Not at all true

9. My classmates in this class accept me.

   Very true   Somewhat true   Not very true   Not at all true

10. I get along with other students in this class.

    Very true   Somewhat true   Not very true   Not at all true

11. The teacher in this class makes me feel important.

    Very true   Somewhat true   Not very true   Not at all true

12. When working in groups I often feel left out.

    Very true   Somewhat true   Not very true   Not at all true

13. I can read the books used in this class.

    Very true   Somewhat true   Not very true   Not at all true

14. The teacher helps us set our own goals for learning from the book.

    Very true   Somewhat true   Not very true   Not at all true

15. My teacher helps me learn from the books in this class.

    Very true   Somewhat true   Not very true   Not at all true

16. Usually I cannot complete the reading for this class.

    Very true   Somewhat true   Not very true   Not at all true

17. The teacher relates the reading to my interests.

    Very true   Somewhat true   Not very true   Not at all true

18. We do projects connected to what we read in this class.

    Very true   Somewhat true   Not very true   Not at all true

19. I say what I think about the topics in the books for this course.

    Very true   Somewhat true   Not very true   Not at all true

20. The reading material in this class does not connect to my world.

    Very true   Somewhat true   Not very true   Not at all true

Thank you.

Teacher Questionnaire for Reading in School

Name _____ **Date** _____

Directions to Teacher

Please answer the items below. It is important to be honest. Make your own decisions about each item. There are no right or wrong answers. This information will NOT be provided to others, unless you approve.

Circle one response for each item under the sentence.

Example:

A. My teaching is important to me.

(Strongly Agree)   Agree   Disagree   Strongly Disagree

If you strongly agree that your teaching is important to you, circle Strongly Agree, as above.

---

1. I place the highest priority on having students explain basic principles.

   Strongly Agree   Agree   Disagree   Strongly Disagree

2. I post unit goals and daily objectives.

   Strongly Agree   Agree   Disagree   Strongly Disagree

3. Student interpretations about the readings are more important than the text itself.

   Strongly Agree   Agree   Disagree   Strongly Disagree

4. In this class, students must recall a lot of factual information.

   Strongly Agree   Agree   Disagree   Strongly Disagree

5. I allow students to select topics for study in this course.

   Strongly Agree   Agree   Disagree   Strongly Disagree

6. Students direct their own learning much of the time.

   Strongly Agree   Agree   Disagree   Strongly Disagree

7. I teach students to take initiative in doing their own reading.

   Strongly Agree   Agree   Disagree   Strongly Disagree

8. This course follows the textbook and the curriculum guide precisely.

   Strongly Agree   Agree   Disagree   Strongly Disagree

9. My group activities interest the students in this class.

   Strongly Agree   Agree   Disagree   Strongly Disagree

10. I ask for student suggestions about how to organize and run this class.

    Strongly Agree   Agree   Disagree   Strongly Disagree

11. Having students exchange viewpoints is important.

    Strongly Agree   Agree   Disagree   Strongly Disagree

12. I believe students learn most when they work on their own.

    Strongly Agree   Agree   Disagree   Strongly Disagree

13. I provide extra texts that help students to understand course content.

    Strongly Agree   Agree   Disagree   Strongly Disagree

14. I help students set their goals for reading.

    Strongly Agree   Agree   Disagree   Strongly Disagree

15. All students can read the books in this course confidently.

    Strongly Agree   Agree   Disagree   Strongly Disagree

16. I do not worry whether students can read the books aloud.

    Strongly Agree   Agree   Disagree   Strongly Disagree

17. I give students hands-on experiences related to the texts.

    Strongly Agree   Agree   Disagree   Strongly Disagree

18. We discuss how this subject relates to everyday life.

    Strongly Agree   Agree   Disagree   Strongly Disagree

19. I help students link the topics of this course to their experiences.

    Strongly Agree   Agree   Disagree   Strongly Disagree

20. I think the texts are the most important part of the course.

    Strongly Agree   Agree   Disagree   Strongly Disagree

Thank you.

Resources

Resource A

Gaps Between Students' Reading Levels and Textbooks

Gaps Between Students' Reading Levels and Textbooks for Grade 8 Students

NAEP Basic Student—Grade 8 (Below-grade level) CANNOT succeed in this reading task

Text sample

For all the hard work that went into building these new homes, the Anasazi did not live in them long. By 1300 A.D. the cliff dwellings were empty. Mesa Verde was deserted and remained a ghost country for almost six hundred years. Were the people driven out of their homes by enemies? No sign of attack or fighting, or even the presence of other tribes has been found.

Archaeologists who have studied the place now believe there are other reasons. Mesa Verde, the beautiful green table, was not longer a good place to live. For one thing, in the second half of the thirteenth century there were long periods of cold and very little rain fell—or else it came at the wrong time of year. Scientists know this from examining the wood used in the cliff dwellings. The growth rings in trees show good and bad growing seasons. But the people had survived drought and bad weather before, so there must have been another reason (excerpted and adapted from Ahmad, Brodsky, Crofts, & Ellis, 1993).

Question

Explain the main two reasons for the Anasazi move.

Typical Textbooks or Texts in Subject Matters—Grade 8

Science—General Science

Electrons Move Throughout a Metal

The scientific understanding of the bonding in metals is that the metal atoms get so close to one another that their outermost energy levels overlap. This allows their valence electrons to move throughout the metal from the energy level of one atom to the energy levels of the atoms nearby. The atoms form a crystal much like the ions associated with ionic bonding. However, the negative charges (electrons) in the metal are free to move about. You can think of a metal as being made up of positive metal ions with enough valence electrons "swimming" about to keep the ions together and to cancel the positive charge of the ions. The ions are held together because metallic bonds extend throughout the metal in all directions (excerpted and adapted from Todd, 2001).

English

Slow Man by J. M. Coetzee

It is indeed true, Elizabeth Costello is a model guest. Bent over the coffee table in the corner on the living room that she has annexed as her own, she spends the weekend absorbed in a hefty typescript, which she seems to be annotating. He does not offer her meals, and she does not ask. Now and again, without a word, she disappears from the flat. What she does with herself he can only guess; perhaps wander the streets of North Adelaide, perhaps sit in a café and nibble a croissant and watch the traffic.

During one of her absences he hunts for the typescript, merely to see what it is, but cannot find it.

"Am I to infer," he says to her on the Sunday evening, "that you have come knocking on my door in order to study me so that you can use me in a book?"

She smiles. "Would that it were so simple, Mr. Rayment."

"Why is it not simple? It sounds simple enough to me. Are you writing a book and putting me in it? Is that what you are doing? If so, what sort of book is it, and don't you think you need my consent first?"

Gaps Between Students' Reading Level and Textbooks for Grade 12 Students

NAEP Basic Student—Grade 12 (Below-grade level) CANNOT succeed in this reading task

Text sample

The above recalls to mind one of the hardest principles in warfare—where your sympathy and humanity are appealed to, and from sense of expediency, you are forbidden to exercise it. After our regiment had been nearly annihilated, and were compelled to retreat under a galling fire, a boy was supporting his dying brother on one arm, and trying to drag him from the field and the advancing foe. He looked at me imploringly and said, "Captain, help him—won't you? Do, Captain, he'll live." I said, "He's shot through the head; don't you see! and can't live—he's dying now." "Oh, no, he ain't, Captain. Don't leave me." I was forced to reply. "The rebels won't hurt him. Lay him down and come, or both you and I will be lost." The rush of bullets and the yells of the approaching enemy hurried me away—leaving the young soldier over his dying brother (Perie, Grigg, & Donahue, 2005).

Question

Each account of the battle of Shiloh gives us information that the other does not. Describe what each account includes that is omitted by the other. Does this mean that both accounts provide a distorted perspective of what happened in the battle?

Typical Textbooks or Texts
in Subject Matters—Grade 12

Science—Physics

If work is done as a charge moves from one point to another in an electric field, or if work is required to move a charge from one point to another, these two points are said to *differ in electric potential. The magnitude of the work is a measure of this difference of potential.* The concept of potential difference is very important in the understanding of electric phenomena. *The potential difference, V, between two points in an electric field is the work done per unit charge as a charge is moved between these points.*

Potential difference *(V)* = <u>work *(W)*</u>
Charge *(q)*

The unit of potential difference in the MKS system is the volt *(v). One* **volt** *is the potential difference between two points in an electric field such that 1 joule of work is done in moving a charge of 1 coulomb between these points* (Williams, Trinklein, & Metcalfe, 1980).

English—"The Death of Ivan Illych" by L. Tolstoy

A sister was married to Baron Gref, who, like his father-in-law, was a Petersburg chinovnik. Ivan Illych had been *le phenix de la famille*, as they used to say. He was neither so chilling and formal as the eldest brother, nor so uncompromising as the youngest. He was the mean between them—an intelligent, lively, agreeable, and polished man. He had studied at the law school with his younger brother, who did not graduate, but was expelled from the fifth class; Ivan Illych, however, finished his course creditably. At the law school he showed the same characteristics by which he was afterward distinguished all his life: he was capable, good-natured even to gayety, and sociable, but strictly fulfilling all that he considered to be his duty; duty, in his opinion, was all that is considered to be such by men in the highest station.

Resource B

Popular, High-Interest Novels That Are Readable

Author	Titles	Themes and Motifs
Sharon Draper	Double Dutch	State exams, bullying, self-reliance
	Forged by Fire	Permanence of the past, protecting the young, foster homes
	Tears of a Tiger	DWI, self-inflicted guilt, isolation, moving on from mistakes
Sharon Flake	The Skin I'm In	Skin tone, bullying, self-acceptance, model teachers
	Begging for Change	Homelessness, guilt from wrong-doing, consequences of one's actions, young love
Angela Johnson	The First Part Last	Teen pregnancy, ethical dilemmas, life priorities
	Looking for Red	Importance of family, loss, fears of the future
Janet McDonald	Spellbound	Teen pregnancy, importance of academics, determination to succeed
	Twists & Turns	HS graduates, working with others, success despite all odds
Walter Dean Myers	Hoops	NBA dreams, ethical dilemmas, life priorities
	The Dream Bearer	Self-discovery, father-son relationships, acceptance of others
Luis Rodriguez	Always Running	Exiting a gang, poverty, racism in America

Resource C

Rubric of Questioning for Personalizing

Questioning Rubric

Level 1: Factual Information

Questions are simple in form and request a simple answer, such as a single fact.

Questions are a request for a factual proposition. They are based on naïve concepts about the world rather than disciplined understanding of the subject matter. Questions refer to relatively trivial, nondefining characteristics of organisms (plants and animals), ecological concepts, or biomes.

- Commonplace or general features of animals that require simple and factual answers: *How big are bats? Do sharks eat trash? How much do bears weigh?*
- Simple classification that only requires a yes/no type of answer or a one-word answer: *Are sharks mammals? What is the biggest shark? Are there male and female polar bears? How many coats of fur do polar bears have?*

Level 2: Simple Description

Questions are a request for a global statement about an ecological concept or an important aspect of survival.

Questions may also request general information that denotes a link between the biome and organisms that live in it. The question may be simple, yet the answer may contain multiple facts and generalizations. The answer may be a moderately complex description or an explanation of an animal's behavior

or physical characteristics. An answer may also be a set of distinctions necessary to account for all the forms of species.

- Ecological concepts in their global characteristics. Usually the ques-
  tion inquires about *how* and *why*, so an explanation can be elicited:
  *How do sharks mate? How do sharks have babies? How do birds
  fly? How do bats protect themselves?*
- A global distinction to classify the animal (general taxonomy). *How
  many types of bats are there? What kinds of sharks are in the ocean?*
- A global distinction or classification about the animal's habitat:
  *What types of places can polar bears live? What kinds of water do
  sharks live in?*
- Simple description of an aspect of an ecological concept: *How many
  eggs does a shark lay? How fast can a bat fly? How far do polar
  bears swim in the ocean?*

Level 3: Complex Explanation

Questions are a request for an elaborated explanation about a specific aspect
of an ecological concept with accompanying evidence.

The question probes the ecological concept by using knowledge about survival or animal biological characteristics. Questions may also request information that denotes a link between the biome and organisms that live in it.
Questions use defining features of biomes to probe for the influence those
attributes have on life in the biome. The question is complex and the
expected answer requires elaborated propositions, general principles and
supporting evidence about ecological concepts.

- An ecological concept of the animal interacting with the environment. The question probes into a specific concept by showing prior
  knowledge on a significant aspect of the interaction: *Why do sharks
  sink when they stop swimming? Why do sharks eat things that bleed?
  How do polar bears keep warm in their dens?* Alternatively, the
  question can address <u>physical characteristics</u> that enable the interaction or biological process to occur: *Why do sharks have three rows
  of teeth? Why is the polar bear's summer coat a different color? Why
  do all bats have sharp teeth?*
- Requests a distinction among types of organisms within a species to
  understand the concept at hand. Either information about the ecological concept or the animals' interaction with the environment is
  used as the basis of an analytical process: *What kinds of sharks lay
  eggs? What kinds of bats hide in caves?* <u>Or,</u> the question may be

directed to a structural or a behavioral characteristic necessary for the concept to be understood: *Do fruit-eating bats have really good eyes? Do owls that live in the desert hunt at night?*

Level 4: Pattern of Relationships

Questions display science knowledge coherently expressed to probe the interrelationship of concepts, the interaction with the biome, or the interdependencies of organisms.

Questions are a request for principled understanding with evidence for complex interactions among multiple concepts and possibly across biomes. Knowledge is used to form a focused inquiry into a specific aspect of a biological concept and an organism's interaction with its biome. Answers may consist of a complex network of two or more concepts.

- Descriptions of animals' survival processes in which two or more ecological concepts are interacting with each other: *Do snakes use their fangs to kill their enemies as well as poison their prey? Do polar bears hunt seals to eat or feed their babies? Why do salmon go to the sea to mate and lay eggs in the river? How do animals and plants in the desert help each other? How does the grassland help the animals in the river? How are grassland animals and river animals the same and different?*

SOURCE: Taboada & Guthrie, 2006

Resource D

Evaluation Rubric

You may use the rubric titled "Curriculum Evaluation Rubric for Reading Engagement" to evaluate your curriculum and instruction. We suggest taking the following six steps. First, identify the unit of curriculum to rate. This may be a one-month segment, or a full year's program. For example, you might select ninth-grade history. Second, identify the level of students you will be considering (above-grade level, at-grade level, slightly below-grade level, or struggling readers below-grade level). For example, you might select the at-grade or slightly below-grade students in this ninth-grade history curriculum. You should conduct the rating for each of these three groups. It is obvious that an instructional program that is motivating and engaging for above-grade students may not be so effective for below-grade students. This is up to your judgment.

Third, examine the unit for evidence that there is guidance for the teacher and support in the materials to perform the instructional practices. Mere opportunity is not sufficient. There should be prompts, activities described, models, student responses stated, and teacher actions specified. These may be optional or expected of teachers. Fourth, rate each practice from –4 to +4. As the scoring guide that follows designates, +4 shows full support for the practice, while –4 shows evidence of activities that preempt the practice. A highly supportive curriculum receives a +4. For example, one that uses "texts at the students' reading level" (as support for self-efficacy) very effectively and consistently receives this high score. Notice that some practices begin with "avoid" in the rubric. If this practice is highly frequent, the score is +4. That score would show that the practice was reasonably motivating because the program does not emphasize rote memorization. In contrast, in the mastery motivation, if the instruction does not clearly *avoid rote recall*, the score would be –3 or –4. This signifies that the practice does not promote mastery learning and is not motivating.

The meanings of each score for each practice are indicated below.

+4 practice is explicitly important, frequently used, appropriately scaffolded, varied

+3 practice is frequently present, but guidance is vague; scaffolding is limited

+2 practice is recommended as an option; brief guidance is given for its use

+1 practice is vaguely suggested, but frequency and scaffolding are low

–1 practice is rarely mentioned; it is an option with low importance

–2 practice is not encouraged nor guided, but it could be added

–3 practice is not explicitly supported; it is crowded out by alternatives

–4 practice is precluded; activities contradict it; students never experience this

Fifth, add the scores for each motivation to get the total for that motivation-support set. The sum for each individual motivation ranges from –16 (most disengaging) to +16 (most engaging). Sixth, add the individual motivation scores to get the total score, which ranges from –80 to +80.

A program of curriculum and instruction with a sum in the negative range (–80 to 0) is placed in the category of Undermining Engagement. It may be demotivating for many students.

A program in the neutral range (1 to 40) is in the area of Limited Engagement. It may be engaging for some students, but it depends substantially on teacher time, effort, and creativity.

A program that is in the positive range (41 to 80) is in the Supporting Engagement category. It is likely to be motivating or to have the potential for engaging a high proportion of students, perhaps with some fine-tuning. Such a program is solid but could be enhanced by adopting and adapting some of the recommended practices more fully.

Curriculum Evaluation Rubric for Reading Engagement

Motivations	Motivation-Supportive Practices in the Curriculum	Score Ranges	Scores
Mastery		−16–+16	
	Students explain principles from text	−4–+4	
	Students relate prior knowledge to text	−4–+4	
	Arrange understanding performances	−4–+4	
	Curriculum avoids rote recall	−4–+4	
Autonomy		−16–+16	
	Students choose text	−4–+4	
	Students input to display of reading comp.	−4–+4	
	Students select subtopics	−4–+4	
	Curriculum avoids overcontrol	−4–+4	
Social		−16–+16	
	Text-based group work is frequent	−4–+4	
	Individuals fully participate in teams	−4–+4	
	Students co-construct reading plans	−4–+4	
	Curriculum avoids peer competition	−4–+4	
Self-Efficacy		−16–+16	
	Texts are at student's reading level	−4–+4	
	Students set reading goals	−4–+4	
	Teacher feedback for self-regulated reading	−4–+4	
	Curriculum avoids difficult texts	−4–+4	
Interest		−16–+16	
	Hands-on activities linked to reading	−4–+4	
	Reading relates to student's experience	−4–+4	
	Students link self to text	−4–+4	
	Curriculum avoids unfamiliar topics	−4–+4	
Total		−80–+80	

+4 practice is explicit, frequently used, appropriately scaffolded, varied
+3 practice is frequently present, but guidance is vague; scaffolding is limited
+2 practice is recommended as an option; brief guidance is given for its use
+1 practice is vaguely suggested, but frequency and scaffolding are low
−1 practice is rarely mentioned; it is an option with low importance
−2 practice is not encouraged nor guided, but it could be added
−3 practice is not explicitly supported; it is crowded out by alternatives
−4 practice is precluded; activities contradict it; students never experience this

Bibliography

Ahmad, I., Brodsky, H., Crofts, M., & Ellis, E. (1993). *World cultures: A global mosaic.* Englewood Cliffs, NJ: Prentice Hall.

Alexander, P., Jetton, T., & Kulikowich, J. (1995). Interrelation of knowledge, interest, and recall: Assessing a model of domain learning. *Journal of Educational Psychology, 87,* 559–575.

Alvermann, D. E. (2001). Reading adolescents' reading identities: Looking back to see ahead. *Journal of Adolescent and Adult Literacy, 44,* 676–690.

Anderman, L. H., & Anderman, E. M. (1999). Social predictors of changes in students' achievement goal orientations. *Contemporary Educational Psychology, 24*(1), 21–37.

Applebee, A. N., Langer, J. A., Nystrand, M., & Gamoran, A. (2003). Discussion-based approaches to developing understanding: Classroom instruction and student performance in middle and high school English. *American Educational Research Journal, 40,* 685–730.

Archer, A. L., Gleason, M. M., & Vachon, V. L. (2003). Decoding and fluency: Foundation skills for struggling older readers. *Learning Disability Quarterly, Special Issue: Effective Instruction for Struggling Secondary Students, 26,* 89–101.

Artlet, C., Baumert, J., Julius-McElvany, N., & Peschar, J. (2003). *Learners for life: Students approaches to learning: Results from PISA 2000.* Paris: OCED.

Assor, A., Kaplan, H., & Kanat-Maymon, Y. (2005). Directly controlling teacher behaviors as predictors of poor motivation and engagement in girls and boys: The role of anger and anxiety. *Learning and Instruction, Special Issue: Feelings and Emotions in the Learning Process, 15,* 397–413.

Assor, A., Kaplan, H., & Roth, G. (2002). Choice is good, but relevance is excellent: Autonomy-enhancing and suppressing teacher behaviors predicting students' engagement in schoolwork. *British Journal of Educational Psychology, 72,* 261–278.

Baker, L., & Wigfield, A. (1999). Dimensions of children's motivation for reading and their relations to reading activity and reading achievement. *Reading Research Quarterly, 34,* 452–477.

Bandura, A. (1997). *Self-efficacy: The exercise of control.* New York: Freeman.

Bean, T., Senior, H., Valerio, P., & White F. (1999). Secondary English students' engagement in reading and writing about a multicultural novel. *Journal of Educational Research, 93,* 32–37.

Best, R. M, Rowe, M., Ozuru, Y., & McNamara, D. S. (2005). Deep-level comprehension of science texts: The role of the reader and the text. *Topics in Language
Disorders, 25,* 65–83.

Bintz, W. P., & Shelton, K. S. (2004). Using written conversation in middle school:
Lessons from a teacher researcher project. *Journal of Adolescent and Adult
Literacy, 47,* 492–507.

Bitz, M. (2004). The comic book project: Forging alternative pathways to literacy.
Journal of Adolescent and Adult Literacy, 47, 574–586.

Boyd, F. B. (2002). Motivation to continue: Enhancing literacy learning for struggling readers and writers. *Reading & Writing Quarterly, 18,* 257–277.

Brophy, J., & Alleman, J. (1991). A caveat: Curriculum integration isn't always a
good idea. *Educational Leadership, 49,* 66.

Brown, D. F. (2002). Self-directed learning in an 8th grade classroom. *Educational
Leadership, 60,* 54–59.

Brozo, W. G., & Hargis, C. H. (2003). Taking seriously the idea of reform: One high
school's efforts to make reading more responsive to all students. *Journal of
Adolescent & Adult Literacy, 47,* 14–23.

Campbell, N. A., Reece, J. B., & Mitchell, L. G. (1999). A tour of the cell. In E.
Mulligan (Eds.), *Biology* (5th ed., p. 103). Glenview, IL: Scott Foresman-
Addison Wesley.

Cappella, E., & Weinstein, R. S. (2001). Turning around reading achievement:
Predictors of high school students' academic resilience. *Journal of Educational
Psychology, 93,* 758–771.

Capri, A. (2003). Chemical reactions. *Vision learning.* Retrieved May 16, 2006,
from http://www.visionlearning.com/library/module_viewer.php?mid=54

Cavelos, J. (1999). *The science of Star Wars: An astrophysicist's independent exam-
ination of space travel, aliens, planets, and robots as portrayed in the Star Wars
films and books.* New York: St. Martin's Press.

Chinn, C. A., Anderson, R. C., & Waggoner, M. A. (2001). Patterns of discourse in
two kinds of literature discussion. *Reading Research Quarterly, 36,* 378–412.

Church, M., Elliot, A., & Gable, S. (2001). Perceptions of classroom environment,
achievement goals, and achievement outcomes. *Journal of Educational
Psychology, 93,* 43–54.

Ciardiello, A. V. (2003). "To wander and wonder": Pathways to literacy and inquiry
through question-finding. *Journal of Adolescent and Adult Literacy, 47,*
228–239.

Coetzee, J. M. (2006). *Slow man.* New York: Vintage Books.

Cohn, M., & Holden, W. (2006). *Behind enemy lines.* New York: Three Rivers Press.

Connell, J. P., & Wellborn, J. G. (1991). Competence, autonomy, and relatedness: A
motivational analysis of self-system processes. In M. R. Gunnar & L. A. Sroufe
(Eds.), *Self processes and development: The Minnesota symposia on child
development* (Vol. 23, pp. 43–78). Hillsdale, NJ: Erlbaum.

Covington, M. V. (2000). Goal theory, motivation, and school achievement: An inte-
grative review. *Annual Review of Psychology, 51,* 171–200.

Coyne, M. D., Kame'enui, E. J., & Simmons, D. C. (2001). Prevention and intervention in beginning reading: Two complex systems. *Learning Disabilities
Research & Practice, 16,* 62–73.

Crane, S. (1990). *The red badge of courage.* New York: Tor Books.

Davis, H. A. (2003). Conceptualizing the role and influence of student-teacher relationships on children's social and cognitive development. *Educational Psychologist, 38,* 207–234.

Deci, E. L. (1992). The relation of interest to the motivation of behavior: A self-determination theory perspective. In K. A. Renniger, S. Hidi, & A. Krapp (Eds.), *The role of interest in learning and development* (pp. 43–70). Hillsdale, NJ: Erlbaum.

Deci, E. L., & Ryan, R. M. (1985). The general causality orientations scale: Self-determination in personality. *Journal of Research in Personality, 19,* 109–134.

Deci, E. L., & Ryan, R. M. (2000). The "what" and "why" of goal pursuits: Human needs and the self-determination of behavior. *Psychology Inquiry, 11,* 227–268.

Delespaul, P. A. E. G., Reis, H. T., & DeVries, M. W. (2004). Ecological and motivational determinants of activation: Studying compared to sports and watching TV. *Social Indicators Research, 67,* 129–143.

Deshler, D. D., Schumaker, J. B., & Lenz, B. K. (2001). Ensuring content-area learning by secondary students with learning disabilities. *Learning Disabilities Research & Practice, 16,* 96–108.

Diakidoy, I. N., Kendeou, P., & Ioannides, C. (2003). Reading about energy: The effects of text structure in science learning and conceptual change. *Contemporary Educational Psychology, 28,* 335–356.

Dole, J. A. (2000). Readers, texts and conceptual change learning. *Reading & Writing Quarterly: Overcoming Learning Difficulties, 16,* 99–118.

Dole, J. A., Brown, K. J., & Trathen, W. (1996). The effects of strategy instruction on the comprehension performance of at-risk students. *Reading Research Quarterly, 31,* 62–84.

Donahue, P. L., Daane, M. C., & Yin, Y. (2005). *The nation's report card: Reading 2003* (Publication No. NCES 2005-453). Washington, DC: U.S. Government Printing Office.

Dowson, M., & McInerney, D. M. (2003). What do students say about their motivational goals? Towards a more complex and dynamic perspective on student motivation. *Contemporary Educational Psychology, 28,* 91–113.

Ehri, L. C. (1995). Phases of development in learning to read words by sight. *Journal of Research in Reading, Special Issue: The Contribution of Psychological Research, 18,* 116–125.

Ehri, L. C., & McCormick, S. (1998). Phases of word learning: Implications for instruction with delayed and disabled readers. *Reading & Writing Quarterly: Overcoming Learning Difficulties, Special Issue: Promoting Word Learning with Delayed Readers, 14,* 135–163.

Eichinger, J. (2003). Tabloid science. *The Science Teacher, 70,* 58–59.

Fink, R. P. (1992). Successful dyslexics' alternative pathways for reading: A developmental study. *Dissertation Abstracts International, 53*(5A), 1461.

Finley, M. (2002). Jedi mind trick: So, you want to be a Jedi, hmmm? *Computer User, 20,* 18.

Finn, J. D. (2001). School noncompletion and literacy. In U.S. Department of Education (Ed.), *Adult literacy and education in America* (pp. 41–71). Washington, DC: National Center for Education Statistics.

Finn, J. D., & Rock, D. A. (1997). Academic success among students at risk for school failure. *Journal of Applied Psychology, 82,* 221–234.

Flowerday, T., & Schraw, G. (2000). Teacher beliefs about instructional choice: A phenomenological study. *Journal of Educational Psychology, 92,* 634–645.

Fredericks, J. A., Blumenfeld, P. C., & Paris, A. H. (2004). School engagement: Potential of the concept, state of the evidence. *Review of Educational Research, 74,* 59–107.

Fuchs, L. S., Fuchs, D., & Kazdan, S. (1999). Effects of peer-assisted learning strategies on high school students with serious reading problems. *Remedial and Special Education, 20,* 309–318.

Fuhler, C. J. (1991). Add sparkle and sizzle to middle school social studies. *Social Studies, 82,* 234–237.

Furrer, C., & Skinner, E. (2003). Sense of relatedness as a factor in children's academic engagement and performance. *Journal of Educational Psychology, 95,* 148–162.

George J. C., & Schoenherr, J. (1972). *Julie of the wolves.* New York: Harper Trophy.

Gnaldi, M., Schagen, I., & Twist, L. (2005). Attitude items and low ability students: The need for a cautious approach to interpretation. *Educational Studies, 31,* 103–113.

Golding, W. (1959). *Lord of the flies.* New York: Perigee Trade.

Goodnough, K., & Cashion, M. (2003). Fostering inquiry through problem-based learning. *Science Teacher, 70,* 21–25.

Gottfried, A. E. (1985). Academic intrinsic motivation in elementary and junior high school students. *Journal of Educational Psychology, 77,* 631–645.

Gottfried, A. E. (1990). Academic intrinsic motivation in young elementary school children. *Journal of Educational Psychology, 82,* 525–538.

Gottfried, A. E., Fleming, J. S., & Gottfried, A. W. (2001). Continuity of academic intrinsic motivation from childhood through late adolescence: A longitudinal study. *Journal of Educational Psychology, 93,* 3–13.

Gottfried, A. W., Cook, C. R., & Gottfried, A. E. (2005). Educational characteristics of adolescents with gifted academic intrinsic motivation: A longitudinal investigation from school entry through early adulthood. *Gifted Child Quarterly, 49,* 172–186.

Greenleaf, C. L., Schoenbach, R., Cziko, C., & Mueller, F. L. (2001). Apprenticing adolescent readers to academic literacy. *Harvard Educational Review, 71,* 79–129.

Grigg, W. S., Daane, M. C., Jin, Y., & Campbell, J. R. (2003). *The nation's report card: Reading 2002* (Publication No. NCES 2003-521). Washington, DC: U.S. Government Printing Office.

Grolnick, W. S., & Ryan, R. M. (1987). Autonomy in children's learning: An experimental and individual difference investigation. *Journal of Personality and Social Psychology, 52,* 890–898.

Grolnick, W. S., Ryan, R. M., & Deci, E. L. (1991). Inner resources for school achievement: Motivational mediators of children's perceptions of their parents. *Journal of Educational Psychology, 83,* 508–517.

Guthrie, J. T. (Ed.) (2008). *Engaging Adolescents in Reading.* Thousand Oaks, CA: Corwin Press.

Guthrie, J. T., & Davis, M. H. (2003). Motivating struggling readers in middle school through an engagement model of classroom practice. *Reading & Writing Quarterly, 19,* 59–85.

Guthrie, J. T., Hoa, L. W. Wigfield, A., Tonks, S. M. Humenick, N. M. & Littles, E. (2007). Reading motivation and reading comprehension growth in the later elementary years. *Contemporary Educational Psychology, 32,* 282–313.

Guthrie, J. T., Schafer, W. D., & Huang, C. W. (2001). Benefits of opportunity to read and balanced instruction on the NAEP. *Journal of Educational Research, 96,* 145–162.

Guthrie, J. T., Schafer, W. D., Wang, Y. Y., & Afflerbach, P. (1995). Relationships of instruction of reading: An exploration of social, cognitive, and instructional connections. *Reading Research Quarterly, 30,* 8–25.

Guthrie, J. T., Wagner, A. L., Wigfield, A., Tonks, S. M., & Perencevich, K. C. (2006). From spark to fire: Can situational reading interest lead to long-term reading motivation? *Reading Research and Instruction, 45,* 85–98.

Guthrie, J. T., Wigfield, A., Humenick, N. M., Perencevich, K. C., Taboada, A., & Barbosa, P. (2006). Influences of stimulating tasks on reading motivation and comprehension. *Journal of Educational Research, 99,* 232–245.

Guthrie, J., Wigfield, A., & Von Secker, C. (2000). Effects of integrated instruction on motivation and strategy use in reading. *Journal of Educational Psychology, 92,* 331–341.

Haynes, J. (2007). *Getting started with English language learners: How educators can meet the challenge.* Alexandria, VA: Association for Supervision and Curriculum Development.

Hidi, S., & Renninger, K. A. (2006). The four-phase model of interest development. *Educational Psychologist, 41,* 111–127.

Hill, K. (2004). Reading at risk: A survey of literary reading in America (Research Report No. 46). Washington, DC: New Vision Communications.

Homer. (1991). *The Iliad.* New York: Penguin Classics.

Homer. (1999). *The Odyssey.* New York: Penguin Putnam.

Ivey, G. (2000). Redesigning reading instruction. *Educational Leadership, 58,* 42–45.

Ivey, G. (2002). Getting started: Manageable literacy practices. *Educational Leadership, 60,* 20–23.

Joyce, B. R., & Showers, B. (1995). *Student achievement through staff development: Fundamentals of school renewal* (2nd ed.). New York: Longman.

Kasser, T., & Ryan, R. M. (1993). A dark side of the American dream: Correlates of financial success as a central life aspiration. *Journal of Personality and Social Psychology, 65,* 410–422.

Kasser, T., & Ryan, R. M. (1996). Further examining the American dream: Differential correlates of intrinsic and extrinsic goals. *Personality and Social Psychology Bulletin, 22,* 280–287.

Kirsch, I., DeJong, J., LaFontaine, D., McQueen, J., Mendelovits, J., & Monseur, C. (2002). *Reading for change: Performance and engagement across countries: Results from PISA 2000* (Publication No. ED474915). Washington, DC: U.S. Government Printing Office.

Klingner, J. K., & Vaughn, S. (1996). Reciprocal teaching of reading comprehension strategies for students with learning disabilities who use English as a second language. *Elementary School Journal, 96*(3), 275–293.

Klingner, J. K., Vaughn, S., Arguelles, M. E., Hughes, M. T., & Leftwich, S. A. (2004). Collaborative strategic reading: "Real-world" lessons from classroom teachers. *Remedial and Special Education, 25,* 291–302.

Kohn, A., Bates, J. A., & Polyson, J. A. (1999). Implementing teaching strategies. In M. E. Ware & C. L. Brewer (Eds.), *Handbook for teaching statistics and research methods* (2nd ed., pp. 179–202). Mahwah, NJ: Erlbaum.

Kuhn, M. R., & Stahl, S. S. (2003). Fluency: A review of developmental and remedial practices. *Journal of Educational Psychology, 95,* 3–21.

Lau, K., & Chan, D. W. (2003). Reading strategy use and motivation among Chinese good and poor readers in Hong Kong. *Journal of Research in Reading, 26,* 177–190.

Lee, H. (1999). *To kill a mockingbird.* Minneapolis, MN: Sagebrush.

Lenz, B. K., & Hughes, C. A. (1990). A word identification strategy for adolescents with learning disabilities. *Journal of Learning Disabilities, 23,* 149–158, 163.

Lepola, J. (2004). The role of gender and reading competence in the development of motivational orientations from kindergarten to grade 1. *Early Education and Development, 15,* 215–240.

Lepola, J., Salonen, P., & Vauras, M. (2000). The development of motivational orientations as a function of divergent reading careers from pre-school to the second grade. *Learning and Instruction, 10,* 153–177.

Lepola, J., Salonen, P., & Vauras, M. (2004). Understanding the development of subnormal performance in children from a motivational-interactionist perspective. In H. N. Switzky (Ed.), *Personality and motivational systems in mental retardation* (Vol. *28,* pp. 145–189). San Diego, CA: Elsevier Academic Press.

Levine, R., Rathbun, A., Selden, R., & Davis, A. (1998). *NAEP's constituents: What do they want? Report of the National Assessment of Educational Progress constituents' survey and focus groups* (Publication No. NCES 98521). Washington, DC: U.S. Government Printing Office.

Liang, L. (2002). On the shelves of the local library: High interest, easy reading trade books for struggling middle and high school reader. *Preventing School Failure, 46,* 183–188.

Linnenbrink, E. A., & Pintrich, P. R. (2002). Motivation as an enabler for academic success. *School Psychology Review, 31,* 1–16.

Linnenbrink, E. A., & Pintrich, P. R. (2003). The role of self-efficacy beliefs in Student engagement and learning in the classroom. *Reading & Writing Quarterly, 19,* 119–137.

Lowry, L. (2002). *The giver.* Minneapolis, MN: Sagebrush.

Lutz, S. L., Guthrie, J. T., & Davis, M. H. (2006). Scaffolding for engagement in elementary school reading instruction. *Journal of Educational Research, 100,* 3–20.

Mac Iver, D., Stipek, D., & Daniels, D. (1991). Explaining within-semester changes in student effort in junior high school and senior high school courses. *Journal of Educational Psychology, 83,* 201–211.

McLaughlin, M., & DeVoogd, G. (2004). Critical literacy as comprehension: Expanding reader response. *Journal of Adolescent and Adult Literacy, 48,* 52–62.

McMaster, K. L., Fuchs, D., & Fuchs, L. S. (2006). Research on peer-assisted learning strategies: The promise and limitations of peer-mediated instruction. *Reading and Writing Quarterly: Overcoming Learning Difficulties, 22,* 5–25.

Meece, J. L., & Holt, K. (1993). A pattern analysis of students' achievement goals. *Journal of Educational Psychology, 93,* 582.

Miserandino, M. (1996). Children who do well in school: Individual differences in perceived competence and autonomy in above average children. *Journal of Educational Psychology, 88,* 203–214.

Moats, L. (2004). Efficacy of a structured, systematic language curriculum for adolescent poor readers. *Reading & Writing Quarterly, 20,* 145–159.

Moje, E. B., Dillon, D. R., & O'Brien, D. (2000). Reexamining roles of learner, text, and context in secondary literacy. *Journal of Educational Research, 93,* 165–180.

Moore, D. W., Bean, T. W., Birdyshaw, D., & Rycik, J. A. (1999). Adolescent literacy: A position statement. *Journal of Adolescent and Adult Literacy, 43,* 97–112.

Moss, B., & Hendershot, J. (2002). Exploring sixth graders' selection of nonfiction trade books. *The Reading Teacher, 56,* 6–17.

Muir, J., & Cornell, J. (2000). *John Muir: My life with nature.* Nevada City, CA: Dawn Publications.

Mullis, I. V. S., Martin, M. O., Gonzalez, E. J., & Kennedy, A. M. (2003). *PIRLS 2001 international report: IEA's study of reading literacy achievement in primary schools in 35 countries.* Data from the International Association for the Evaluation of Educational Achievement (IEA), Progress in International Reading Literacy Study, 2001. NAEP, 2003, Princeton, NJ: Educational Testing Service.

Myers, W. D. (1983). *Hoops.* New York: Laurel Leaf.

Myers, W. D. (1999). *Monster.* New York: Amistad.

Nichols, W. D., Jones, J. P., & Hancock, D. R. (2003). Teachers' influence on goal orientation: Exploring the relationship between eighth graders' goal orientation, their emotional development, their perceptions of learning, and their teachers' instructional strategies. *Reading Psychology, 24,* 57–85.

O'Connor, R., Bell, K., Harty, K., Larkin, L., Sackor, S., & Zigmond, N. (2002). Teaching reading to poor readers in the intermediate grades: A comparison of text difficulty. *Journal of Educational Psychology, 94,* 474–485.

Oravec, J. A. (2002). Bookmarking the world: Weblog applications in education. *Journal of Adolescent and Adult Literacy, 45,* 616–621.

Orwell, G. (1961). *1984.* New York: New American Library.

Orwell, G. (1974). *Animal farm.* New York: New American Library.

Otis, N., Grouzet, F. M. E., & Pelletier, L. G. (2005). Latent motivational change in an academic setting: A 3-year longitudinal study. *Journal of Educational Psychology, 97,* 170–183.

Patterson, P. O., & Elliott, L. N. (2006). Struggling reader to struggling reader: High school students' responses to a cross-age tutoring program. *Journal of Adolescent and Adult Literacy, 49,* 378–389.

Perie, M., Grigg, W. S., & Donahue, P. L. (2005). *The nation's report card: Reading 2005* (Publication No. NCES 2006-451). Washington, DC: U.S. Government Printing Office.

Pikulski J. J., & Chard, D. J. (2005). Fluency: Bridge between decoding and reading comprehension. *Reading Teacher, 58*(6), 510–519.

Pintrich, P. R. (2000). Multiple goals, multiple pathways: the role of goal orientation in learning and achievement. *Journal of Educational Psychology, 92,* 544–555.

Porter, L. A. (2003). *Connecting with the past: Uncovering clues in primary source documents*. Retrieved April 12, 2004, from http://findarticles.com/p/articles/mi_go1689/is_200311/ai_n6524196

Rasinski, T. V., Padak, N. D., McKeon, C. A., Wilfong, L. G., Friedauer, J. A., & Heim, P. (2005). Is reading fluency a key for successful high school reading? *Journal of Adolescent & Adult Literacy, 49,* 22–27.

Reeve, J., & Jang, H. (2006). What teachers say and do to support students' autonomy during a learning activity. *Journal of Educational Psychology, 98,* 209–218.

Reeve, J., Jang, H., Carrell, D., Jeon, S., & Barch, J. (2004). Enhancing students' engagement by increasing teachers' autonomy support. *Motivation and Emotion, 28,* 147–169.

Reynolds, P. L., & Symons, S. (2001). Motivational variables and children's text search. *Journal of Educational Psychology, 93,* 14–23.

Roe, M. F. (1997). Combining enablement and engagement to assist students who do not read and write well. *Middle School Journal, 28,* 35–41.

Rozendaal, J. S., Minnaert, A., & Boekaerts, M. (2005). The influence of teacher perceived administration of self- regulated learning on students' motivation and information-processing. *Learning and Instruction, 15,* 141–160.

Ruddell, M. R. (1995). Literacy assessment in middle level grades: Alternatives to traditional practices. *Reading & Writing Quarterly: Overcoming Learning Difficulties, 11,* 187–200.

Ryan, A. M., Patrick, H., & Shim, S. O. (2005). Differential profiles of students identified by their teacher as having avoidant, appropriate, or dependent help-seeking tendencies in the classroom. *Journal of Educational Psychology, 97,* 275–285.

Ryan, R. M., & Deci, E. L. (2000a). Intrinsic and extrinsic motivations: Classic definitions and new directions. *Contemporary Educational Psychology, 25,* 54–67.

Ryan, R. M., & Deci, E. L. (2000b). Self-determination theory and the facilitation of intrinsic motivation, social development, and well-being. *American Psychologist, 55,* 68–78.

Sachs, M. (1995). *Call me Ruth.* New York: Harper Trophy.

Schiefele, U., & Krapp, A. (1996). Topic interest and free recall of expository text. *Learning and Individual Differences, 8,* 141–160.

Schiefele, U. (1996). Topic interest, text representation, and quality of experience. *Contemporary Educational Psychology, 21,* 3–18.

Schumaker, J. B., & Deshler, D. D. (1988). Implementing the regular education initiative in secondary schools: A different ball game. *Journal of Learning Disabilities, 21,* 36–42.

Schumaker, J. B., Deshler, D. D., & McKnight, P. (2002). Ensuring success in the secondary general education curriculum through the use of teaching routines. In M. R. Shinn, H. M. Walker, & G. Stoner (Eds.), *Interventions for academic and behavior problems II: Preventive and remedial approaches* (pp. 791–823). Washington, DC: National Association of School Psychologists.

Schunk, D. H. (2003). Self-efficacy for reading and writing: Influence of modeling, goal setting, and self-evaluation. *Reading & Writing Quarterly: Overcoming Learning Difficulties, 19,* 159–172.

Schunk, D. H., & Zimmerman, B. J. (1997). Developing efficacious readers and writers: The role of social and self-regulatory processes. In J. T. Guthrie &

A. Wigfield (Eds.), *Reading engagement: Motivating readers through integrated instruction* (pp. 34–50). Newark, DE: International Reading Association.

Seifert, T. L., & O'Keefe, B. A. (2001). The relationship of work avoidance and learning goals to perceived competence, externality and meaning. *British Journal of Educational Psychology, 71,* 81–92.

Shakespeare, W. (2004a). *Julius Caesar.* New York: Washington Square Press.

Shakespeare, W. (2004b). *The taming of the shrew.* New York: Washington Square Press.

Sheldon, K. M., Elliot, A. J., Kim, Y., & Kasser, T. (2001). What is satisfying about satisfying events? Testing 10 candidate psychological needs. *Journal of Personality and Social Psychology, 80,* 325–339.

Singer, J., & Hubbard, R. S. (2002). Teaching from the heart: Guiding adolescent writers to literate lives. *Journal of Adolescent and Adult Literacy, 46,* 326–336.

Skinner, E. A., & Belmont, M. J. (1993). Motivation in the classroom: Reciprocal effects of teacher behavior and students engagement across the school year. *Journal of Educational Psychology, 85,* 571–581.

Skinner, E. A., Wellborn, J. G., & Connell, J. P. (1990). What it takes to do well in school and whether I've got it: A process model of perceived control and children's engagement and achievement in school. *Journal of Educational Psychology, 82,* 22–32.

Sprague, M., & Cotturone, J. (2003). Motivating students to read physics content. *The Science Teacher, 70,* 24–29.

Stanovich, K. E., & Cunningham, A. E. (1992). Studying the consequences of literacy within a literate society: The cognitive correlates of print exposure. *Memory & Cognition, 20,* 51–68.

Stanovich, K., West, R., & Harrison, M. (1995). Knowledge growth and maintenance across the life span: The role of print exposure. *Developmental Psychology, 31,* 811–826.

Stipek, D. (2002). *Motivation to learn: Integrating theory and practice.* Boston: Allyn and Bacon.

Stipek, D. (2004). *Engaging schools: Motivating high school students to learn.* Washington, DC: National Academy of Sciences.

Stone, B., & Brady, S. (1995). Evidence for phonological processing deficits in less-skilled readers. *Annals of Dyslexia, 45,* 51–78.

Stoppard, T. (1991). *Rosencrantz and Guildenstern are dead.* New York: Grove Press.

Sweet, A. P., Guthrie, J. T., & Ng, M. (1998). Teacher perceptions and student reading motivation. *Journal of Educational Psychology, 90,* 210–224.

Taboada, A., & Guthrie, J. T. (2004). Growth of cognitive strategies for reading comprehension. In J. Guthrie, A. Wigfield, & K. Perencevich (Eds.), *Motivating reading comprehension: Concept-Oriented Reading Instruction* (pp. 273–306). Mahwah, NJ: Erlbaum.

Taboada, A., & Guthrie, J. T. (2006). Contributions of student questioning and prior knowledge to construction of knowledge from reading information text. *Journal of Literacy Research, 38,* 1–35.

Taboada, A., Guthrie, J. T., & McRae, A. (in press). Building engaging classrooms: Motivating students daily. In R. Fink & S. J. Samuels (Eds.), *Inspiring success: Reading interest and motivation in an age of high-stakes testing.*

Taylor, B. M., Pearson P. D., & Peterson, D. S. (2003). Reading growth in high-poverty classrooms: The influence of teacher practices that encourage cognitive engagement in literacy learning. *Elementary School Journal, 104,* 3–28.

Thorkildsen, T. A. (2002). Literacy as a lifestyle: Negotiating the curriculum to facilitate motivation. *Reading & Writing Quarterly, 18,* 321–341.

Todd, R. W. (2001). *Physical science.* New York: Holt Rinehart & Winston.

Tolstoy, L. (2003). *The death of Ivan Illych and other stories.* New York: Signet Classics.

Tonks, S. M., Taboada, A., Wigfield, A., & Guthrie, J. T. (2007). Effects of motivational and cognitive variables on reading comprehension. Manuscript in preparation.

Torgesen, J. (2004). Lessons learned from research on interventions for students who have difficulty learning to read. In P. McCardle & V. Chhabra. *The voice of evidence in reading research* (pp. 164–193). Baltimore: Brookes.

Turner, J., Meyer, D., Cox, K., Logan, C., DiCintio, M., & Thomas, C. (1998). Creating contexts for involvement in mathematics. *Journal of Educational Psychology, 90,* 758–771.

Twist, L., Gnaldi, M., & Schagen, I. (2004). Good readers but at a cost? Attitudes to reading in England. *Journal of Research in Reading, 27,* 387–400.

Unrau, N., & Schlackman, J. (2006). Motivation and its relationship with reading achievement in an urban middle school. *Journal of Educational Research, 100,* 81–101.

Urdan, T. (2004). Predictors of academic self-handicapping and achievement: Examining achievement goals, classroom goal structures, and culture. *Journal of Educational Psychology, 96,* 251–264.

Vallerand, R. J., & Bissonnette, R. (1992). Intrinsic, extrinsic, and amotivational styles as predictors of behavior: A prospective study. *Journal of Personality, 60,* 599–620.

Vansteenkiste, M., Lens, W., & Deci, E. L. (2006). Intrinsic versus extrinsic goal contents in self-determination theory: Another look at the quality of academic motivation. *Educational Psychologist, 41,* 19–32.

Vansteenkiste, M., Simons, J., Lens, W., Soenens, B., & Matos, L. (2005). Examining the motivational impact of intrinsic versus extrinsic goal framing and autonomy-supportive versus internally controlling communication style on early adolescents' academic achievement. *Child Development, 76,* 483–501.

Wang, J. H., & Guthrie, J. T. (2004). Modeling the effects of intrinsic motivation, extrinsic motivation, amount of reading, and past reading achievement on text comprehension between U.S. and Chinese students. *Reading Research Quarterly, 39,* 162–186.

Watson, S. (2004). Opening the science doorway. *The Science Teacher, 71,* 32–35.

Weiner, B. (1994). Integrating social and personal theories of achievement striving. *Review of Educational Research, 64,* 557–573.

Wentzel, K. (1996). Social and academic motivation in middle school: Concurrent and long-term relations to academic effort. *Journal of Early Adolescence, 16,* 390–406.

Wentzel, K. R. (1991). Social competence at school: Relation between social responsibility and academic achievement. *Review of Educational Research, 61,* 1–24.

Werderich, D. E. (2002). Individualized responses: Using journal letters as a vehicle for differentiated reading instruction. *Journal of Adolescent and Adult Literacy, 45,* 746–754.

Wiesel, E. (1982). *Night.* New York: Bantam Books.

Wigfield, A. (2004). Motivating for reading during the early adolescent and adolescent years. In D. S. Strickland & D. Alvermann (Eds.), *Bridging the literacy achievement gap (Grades 4–12)* (pp. 56-70). Newark, DE: International Reading Association.

Wigfield, A., Eccles, J. S., Mac Iver, D., Reuman, D. A., & Midgley, C. (1991). Transitions during early adolescence: Changes in children's domain-specific self-perceptions and general self-esteem across the transition to junior high school. *Developmental Psychology, 27,* 552–565.

Wigfield, A., & Guthrie, J. T. (1997). Relations of children's motivation for reading to the amount and breadth of their reading. *Journal of Educational Psychology, 89,* 420–432.

Wilkinson, I. (2006). *Varieties of social interaction during literacy instruction.* Paper presented at The Literacy Institute, Berkeley, CA.

Williams, B. T. (2006). Metamorphosis hurts: Resistant students and myths of transformation. *Journal of Adolescent and Adult Literacy, 50,* 148–153.

Williams, J., Trinklein, F., & Metcalfe, H. (1980). *Modern physics.* New York: Holt Rinehart & Winston.

Yolen, J. (1999). *Encounter.* Tempe, AZ: Sagebrush.

Zahorik, J. (1996). Elementary and secondary teachers' reports of how they make learning interesting. *Elementary School Journal, 96,* 551–564.

Zimmerman, B. J., & Kitsantas, A. (2002). Acquiring writing revision and self-regulatory skill through observation and emulation. *Journal of Educational Psychology, 94,* 660–668.

Index